Middle CHILD

Wanda Coley

BBP
Bilbo Books Publishing
ATHENS, GEORGIA

MIDDLE CHILD

ISBN 978-0-9800108-2-4   0-9800108-2-9

All rights reserved. Published in the United States of America by
Bilbo Book Publishers, Athens, Georgia.

www.bilbobooks.com

To David and Lois,
in loving memory of
Roger, Paul, Mom and Dad

ON THE COVER

Background: Aerial view of the Bjornlie farm in Dawson, Minnesota, circa 1955; Wanda's profound interest in writing is demonstrated at the early age of eight years old, winning grand prize at the 1947 Minnesota State Fair for a story about a family trip to South Dakota.

Inset: Roger, David, Wanda, Paul and Lois Bjornlie in Dawson, Minnesota, circa 1946.

ACKNOWLEDGMENTS

Having embarked on this writing venture, I was fortunate to have received important facts and support from family members.

I am grateful for the interest and support afforded to me by my brother, Dave, and my sister, Lois. They read and discussed with me the content of my writing, and, most importantly, gave me the go-ahead to publish what I had created.

My heartfelt thanks go out to my late cousin, Russell, for his research into the ancestry of my mother's family reaching back into the early 1600's in Norway. His son, Tom, also shared with me the many pictures that Russell had collected of family members that we have in common. Thank you, Tom, for sharing.

My final edits were made so much easier by Tracy, my lovely and talented daughter whose ideas and skills gave me the assurance that I was on the right track. I had planned this as a gift to you and the family, but your gift of partnership in my endeavor is so much bigger. Tracy, I thank you!

Special thanks to William E. Bray and Bowen Craig of Bilbo Books who encouraged and promoted my work during the writing process. Without the two of them, I may not have actually had the courage to fulfill my goal of a written family history. I appreciate their friendship along with their professional assistance.

Thank you, Sarah "Sallie" Krickel, for your editing input. Your comments were invaluable.

Of course, the conversations with family members contributed to the basis of my story. Thanks to cousins, Gerda Dolman and Aletrice Nerassen. Also, thanks to childhood friend and guardian of the farm where my life began, Joann Roisen. Nostalgia at its best!

Lastly, I appreciate the meeting accommodations provided to my group by Two Story Coffee House of East Athens and Loco's of Athens (East Side), and special thanks to Iris Place for allowing all of us in the Writer's Group to meet in one of their rooms. And thanks to the members of Bilbo Writer's Group for your friendship and support.

CONTENTS

INTRODUCTION

Several attempts over the past ten years or so have finally brought me to the right time and place to collect the parts and pieces of my life from my earliest recollections. I have tried to gather these memories into one place to be viewed only from my perspective. Some of the incidents recorded here may not be exactly the way others remember them, but they are a truthful and honest telling of the way things happened as I recall them. I have tried to show cases where my siblings remember some of the instances differently from what I remember. I respect that, but I still want to remain true to the way I have stored these events in my mind. Some of these are funny stories, some not so funny and some a little sad. But I have tried not to make anyone uncomfortable with the telling of family stories.

As changes occurred in my life following the death of my husband after a short illness, I realized that I am who I am and found that I am quite satisfied, most of the time, with myself. I have always had an abundance of independence and self-assurance, but only recently do I feel that I have been tested in those merits, if that is what they are. I can be opinionated if not vocally, at least inwardly. Sometimes I am more critical of myself than I am of others, acknowledging that I have more than my share of faults and inadequacies. I feel these attributes come from my mother, who, although a loving wife and mother, also had an enormous sense of self and purpose. I see my mother and myself in my daughter and can honestly say that she wears these characteristics well.

My mantra is, "I agree to disagree, but will respect the opinions and beliefs of others."

I regret not having many direct references to my ancestors that would have included personal stories and hopes and dreams. I can only deduce from what I know that they were a strong, resourceful, ambitious and loving group of people. I am proud to call these people my family, with all of the little quirks and fallacies of human beings. I hope that my words will find a place in the future generations of my family.

From the age of five I grew up knowing that my place in the family was that of first girl and the middle child. There was a period between the death of my oldest brother, Roger, and until my youngest brother, Paul, died, that I didn't have any reason to think of myself as anything other than one of two sisters to my two brothers. Now, I realize, sadly, that I am once again the Middle Child with the loss of my second brother. Is that a remarkable position to hold? Of course it is only significant to me, as I feel the warmth and love from my brother and sister who define me not by age but by the memories that we share. Who could have known that the crazy times we shared growing up would bring such joy to us, when one of us would say, "Do you remember when?"

❧

AN OVERVIEW

❧

Growing up as I did in the forties and fifties, I realize that I followed the example of my parents and never quite got over the underlying need to save and preserve everything. We were taught by example not to throw anything away that had even the most remote possible use remaining in it. We wore hand-me-downs until we wore holes in them. If the holes couldn't be patched, the buttons were cut off and the material used for cleaning rags to clean floors, cars, stove tops or anything else that needed cleaning. The buttons were relegated to the button box to be used later to replace a lost shirt button or to use on a new dress Mom would make us. Today, I have a difficult time simply discarding seldom or never used items. When I finally realize that some of the things I am debating about are not suitable for donation, I can usually then let go. Yet I still see the need for cloth rags and, in fact, if the fabrics in the discarded clothing were all cotton or wool, I would have a very large rag bag.

I don't want to sound as though I was in any way neglected during this period of my young life. Actually, I know now and knew then, that I was very much loved and spoiled to the extent that was possible. My siblings and I were all shown a lot of attention. We were taught to be respectful and kind but we were also honored on our birthdays and other special occasions. Although we didn't always have a big party on our day, with a family our size we didn't need a bunch of neighborhood kids to feel special. My brother Dave and I had birthdays two years plus one day apart. Tradition in our family called for an angel food cake with fluffy white icing.

The year we turned seven and nine when plans were being made for our cake, my brother and I thought that we should each have our own cake. My mother baked the usual white angel food cake for my brother, and the next day she baked a chocolate angel food cake for me. How special is that?

Being the oldest girl you would have imagined that I would have had all new clothes, but I did have a few older cousins whose dresses ended up in the closet where my dresses were hung. Granted, the cousins were several years older than I, so their dresses were a little outdated. I remember one dress in particular that I had to wear to school when my dresses had not been washed. This was when Mom was sick and had help. Nothing seemed to run as well without Mom in charge. The dress I was told to wear was a size too big and I remember thinking it was really drab. Somehow we all survived and perhaps were made better learning these lessons in humility and adjusting to the circumstances. In retrospect, my brothers and I had both of our parents to guide and care for us, unlike my sister, Lois, who was being cared for by Aunt Laura and Uncle Rob at the time. If I had realized that my baby sister, in the meantime, was being loved and adored, not to mention spoiled, by our aunt and uncle, I would most likely have been really depressed!

Later, when Mom had fully recovered from her appendectomy, phlebitis and the death of her youngest daughter in childbirth, things began to seem a whole lot brighter on all fronts. When my cousin, Arnold, returned from the army in the Philippines and his engagement was announced, I was asked to be a flower girl in his wedding. My cousin, Sally, and I were dressed in pretty long pink dresses and I felt really special. I was even taken to the beauty shop to have my long blonde hair curled into long locks.

As a teenager, clothing fads were coming at us from everywhere. Boys all wanted black leather jackets like James Dean, although I only knew one or two who actually had one of those. Some of the girls were getting poodle skirts. I didn't have one and don't recall ever desiring one. But I did want and get saddle shoes, penny loafers and later white bucks. Some of the boys had blue suede shoes in Elvis Presley style. In the fifties, we wore dresses to school every day except Fridays when we could dress casually in slacks or blue jeans. I realize that fashions are just as or more important today, but the style is so different. Boys in my youth would not have gotten outside the house without a belt to keep their britches at the waist. At the same time, girls would have covered a whole lot more of their bodies. The only time we would see a girl's shoulder would be when she was in her prom dress or a sundress.

Downtown Dawson, MN 1950s

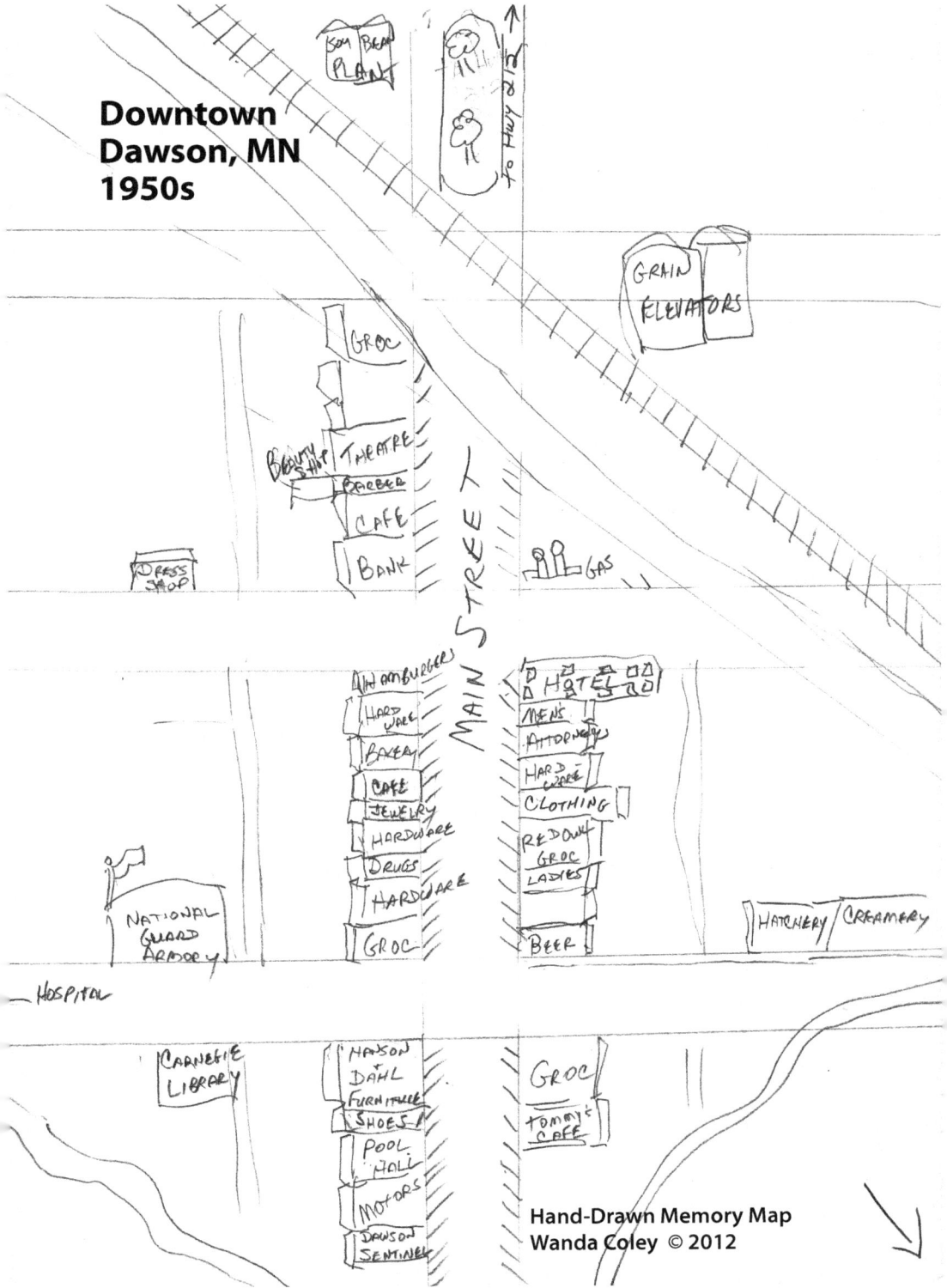

SOY BEAN PLANT

to Hwy 212

GRAIN ELEVATORS

GROC

BEAUTY SHOP

THEATRE

BARBER

CAFE

BANK

DRESS SHOP

GAS

MAIN STREET

HAMBURGER

HARD WARE

BAKERY

CAFE

JEWELRY

HARDWARE

DRUGS

HARDWARE

GROC

HOTEL

MENS

ANTIQUES

HARD WARE

CLOTHING

RED OWL GROC

LADIES

BEER

NATIONAL GUARD ARMORY

HATCHERY / CREAMERY

HOSPITAL

CARNEGIE LIBRARY

HANSON + DAHL FURNITURE

SHOES

POOL HALL

MOTORS

DAWSON SENTINEL

GROC

TOMMY'S CAFE

Hand-Drawn Memory Map
Wanda Coley © 2012

Downtown Dawson, MN Present Day

Walnut St

Co Hwy

5th St

7th St

Dawson Sentinel

Wold Real Estate Agency

600

Miller Services

Rusty Duck Bar & Grill

6th St

5th St

7th St

4th St

Dawson Public Library

800

Pine St

Courtesy Google Maps

My Early Years
The First-Born Girl in the Family

⁓⁓

What is that face on the wall? It is summer time and it is barely light enough in my bedroom to see and remember where I am. The bedroom faces the east and the light coming in the window is shining on the chimney cover on the opposite wall that I face from my bed. Being the only girl at that time, I have a room to myself. My older brothers, Roger and David, share a room across the hall. I am very quiet, trying to make out the face. Finally, the sun comes up and I can recognize a painted outdoor scene on the chimney cover and the face melts into trees in the picture. I feel safe again. Things are not always what they seem to be at first and I will not be afraid of my imagination. I must be three years old or so, as Paul is a baby and sleeps in the crib. Later, I remember Alice coming to stay with us to help Mom in the evenings. She would get off the school bus at our driveway, help with the evening chores, and catch the bus to go to high school in the morning.

I don't remember too much about what Alice did exactly. She was referred to as our "hired girl." Her family lived not far from our house and, as far as I know, she would go home on Friday after school and come back the next Monday when the bus would drop her off at our driveway. I do remember that she painted a chicken wishbone with red nail polish, made a hole in the top, and put a ribbon through the hole so I could wear it around my neck. I don't have any recollection of ever seeing a necklace like this again. It may have been that Alice thought it would be a neat thing to do. The next morning, I asked

Alice for the necklace and Alice ran back up to her room to get it for me. As a result, she missed the bus and Dad had to drive twelve miles to Dawson to take her to school. Someone must have become pretty upset since I remember this little incident so vividly. Apparently, I must have felt considerable guilt about my part in the disruption of the morning. I suppose that Mom would have reminded me that I should not have been so demanding of Alice.

My brothers must have gotten awfully tired of having their little sister tagging around behind them while they played boy games. It was pointed out over and over again that I was a girl, as if I didn't know that. A favorite sport of my brothers was playing Superman and Captain Marvel with dish towels around their necks and running so fast they could almost believe they could fly. I remember joining them as Wonder Woman. How did they think they could get away from me?

A time I shall never forget, was when my insistence in joining them at play left a memory that remains firmly imbedded in my head. It was in the fall of the year, one evening after supper, when we were out in the trees that formed a windbreak near the house. The boys found a nest of chicken eggs in the grass. The nest had been abandoned by a hen when the eggs refused to hatch. Needless to say, these eggs had gotten pretty seasoned when we found them. Roger and David used the eggs to throw at trees to watch them explode. Harmless fun, eh? Not so much when I got too close and was spattered with ripe eggs. I'm sure that we all got a little messed up, but I don't remember getting a spanking. Of course, I was "little miss innocent," but the brothers were older and were in big trouble. I know that the brown and yellow plaid coat that I was wearing that evening wasn't seen after that day. The coat was really pretty ugly, so maybe losing the use of it was a blessing in disguise.

I guess all little boys left on their own for longer than a few minutes are going to get into something they shouldn't, and my brothers were good at it. I can't remember the time they decided to go for a barrel ride down the gentle slope that went from the house to the barn, but I heard the story over and over many times, perhaps as a warning to anyone listening, so just such a thing would not happen ever again. The barrel that appealed to them as a carnival ride was the barrel that held coal in it during the winter months. It was empty, so what was the harm in a little fun? My older brother, Roger, got David to get inside the barrel while he kept the barrel rolling down the hill. No one got hurt during the ride, but both of the boys got a spanking neither one of them forgot after they came back covered in black coal dust. It must have been incidents like this that prompted organized activities such as Boy Scouts, 4-H clubs, Little League baseball and summer camps.

I believe that my love for stories all began with dreams I had as a child. I know that we were read to before we learned to read, but some of the biggest adventures I felt as a small child came to me in dreams. Some of my dreams were fueled by stories from books, but became even more real when the stories were viewed in dreams. I remember to this day a dream I had as a very small child of a band of Indians near the cornfield that edged the front yard. I can still see them walking out of sight toward the farm to the east in their leather and feathers, straight from a storybook. They appeared, in my dream, to be slowly moving on foot, single file, unconcerned about their surroundings. Could they have felt the need to move out of the way of the white intruders who had taken over land they had occupied for generations? Dreams can be confusing. It seemed that I was a part of the picture, yet had no part in their lives. I was not frightened, but fascinated by the picture that emerged from my head.

My mother's father died when I was a year old, so my only recollection of him is from pictures. After he died, my grandmother would come to stay with us for periods of time, perhaps for days or for a week or two. I remember that she was available to us a good bit of the time. I can still smell the molasses cookies she made for us and I picture her sitting on the steps leading to upstairs from the kitchen with the mixing bowl in her lap and a wooden spoon in her hand. I was more than likely about four years old at this time and can still feel the warmth and love from Grandma. I loved her, too and I recall the brown sweet cheese that she loved, so of course I thought it was really great, too. I have thought about the brown cheese often over the years, not knowing how it is made. Research has revealed that this Norwegian cheese is called burnost and is made by boiling whey, milk and cream until it caramelizes into the sweet brown cheese that is almost like candy, but is used to spread on bread or waffles, much like honey or syrup. Kept cool, it is firm. It quickly softens at room temperature. I do remember getting almost sick by eating too much of the cheese by itself. This grandmother, Rebecca Dahl, died when I was five years old and I'm thankful for the wonderful memories of her. I only wish I had more of them.

I guess that our short time with Grandma was mutually beneficial. Grandma didn't have to be alone as she entertained us little ones. I like to think that Mom and Grandma had the opportunity to get the years back that they lost when my mother was a little girl and lived with Mom's sister, Nora. Grandma looked after us little ones while Mom cooked, cleaned, washed, scrubbed and ironed for the grow- ing family. Grandma made whistles for us in the spring from the new shoots of willow trees when they were green and supple. I don't know the exact way she did it, but it involved a paring knife and slipping the green bark from the wood. As I recall, after the bark was taken off the branch, a notch was made in it and then slipped back onto the branch. Somehow, by blowing and sliding the bark back and forth, a magical musical sound would be heard. The whistle looked somewhat like a recorder.

I also remember my mother on the rare occasions she was able to just relax, sitting on the lawn while we picked sweet clover out of the grass. She would weave the stems and flowers into necklaces and crowns for our heads. I remember thinking that these were wonder- ful things created just by using your hands and the supplies given to us by nature. I have been reminded of those days, when my children and grandchildren have brought me dandelions. Aren't we glad to be reminded by little children of the beauty in the simplest things?

Usually we children had to stay at home when Mom went in to town to shop. If we behaved properly, we were rewarded with little boxes of raisins or, better yet, boxes of Cracker Jacks with prizes in the bottom. I always preferred the Cracker Jacks so I could have the sur- prise in the box. The special days were when I got the really nice sur- prise of a new paper doll book. Maybe not all little girls liked paper dolls as much as I did. I was too little to handle scissors at first, so my mother cut them out for me. I thought they were so pretty with the changes of clothes, especially the bride dolls and I would spend hours

on the front screened-in porch, dressing and undressing the paper
dolls and talking for them. What a wonderful world is make believe!
I have no idea what my brothers were up to while I played with my
dolls. They may have been big enough to have chores to do or maybe
they were riding the pony. Or maybe they were playing cowboys and
Indians.

Remembering the paper dolls and the entertainment they provided brings to mind the times when I spent the night at Grandma's
house. I particularly remember one visit when my cousin Robert's
daughter, Marlowe, came to Grandma's house while I was there.
I don't know the reason for her visit. She may have been invited
to come by Grandma's to keep me company or she may just have
dropped in, as they lived not far from Grandma's house. She was several years older than I, perhaps four or five years older, and I sensed
that she was being bossy and I really didn't like her attitude. The way
I remember it, I had my paper dolls with me, or maybe she brought
her dolls with her, but she was beginning to be too controlling and
we had some words. Until Grandma stepped in, that is, and Marlowe
was sent home. Yahoo! I had Grandma to myself again.

The nicest thing about Grandma's house was the smell of food in
the kitchen. When I see an old metal kitchen cabinet in an antique
shop now, I have to open the sugar drawer to see if I can smell the
sugar in it. Something about storing sugar in a metal cabinet gives it
the most delicious aroma, like sugar cookies mixed up in a big bowl
with a wooden spoon and baked with love.

Grandma had made a quilt, pillow and sheets for my wicker doll
carriage. My first and prettiest doll was left in the buggy outside one
summer night and it just so happened to rain during the night. The
face of the doll had cracks in it as a result of the overnight rain. It was
devastating to see my doll ruined that way and, on top of that, to be
scolded for leaving my toys out overnight. This left a lasting impression on me. I don't remember being so careless with my toys ever
again. This may have been the same doll that shared a ginger cookie
with me while sitting on the steps of the front porch. The cookie was
in all probability made by one of my grandmothers, as they were both
really good cookie baking experts. What I do know for certain is that
the doll's little red tongue got pretty messed up with brown molasses

cookie. Did I get scolded for that? I don't remember.

Roger and David had a real talent for getting into trouble. Besides the coal barrel incident and the rotten egg incident, there was the time that they decided to imitate farming and filled the little red wagon with hay (grass clippings). They then tied the handle of the wagon with a rope and tied the other end to the Shetland pony's saddle horn. The only problem was that the wagon came up and hit the back legs of the pony every time the pony moved forward. This resulted in the horse taking off at top speed into the trees with the two boys running behind yelling for the pony to stop. This caused the pony to run even faster. That is, until the wagon didn't make the turn with the pony and was snagged on a tree. Then the poor scared pony had to stop. I recall seeing pieces of the wagon left in the woods. The wheels and handle had been separated from the rest of the wagon.

We had a pony named Lady. Believe me, she was no lady. She was a little on the mean side, in fact. We didn't have her very long, mainly because of the time when Aunt Clara was trying to help one of my brothers up onto the back of the pony and Lady turned around to bite Aunt Clara in the arm. This was not a happy scene. Lady was traded for Captain, the exact opposite of Lady. Lady was brown, whereas Captain was black and white and male. He was absolutely the most gentle of ponies. He stayed with us until we had all outgrown him and he lived until he was 33 or 34 years old with new owners. We were told that they buried him under an apple tree on their farm.

I can still picture in my mind the farm that we lived on, my first home. I can describe for you the layout of the rooms in the house and where the furniture was placed and the location of the telephone on the wall. The telephone was an important feature in a house out in the country where nobody could hear you call for help without a telephone. I see it over the spot on the wall where my brother's highchair stood when not in use. Oh, yes, I gained another brother when I was not quite three years old. My dad had a desk and I can tell you exactly where its place was in the dining room. This was where Dad would sit to keep the accounts of the farm operation. That's where he was working when I had just learned to walk and stumbled, falling headlong into the leg of the chair that Dad was sitting on. A big egg appeared on my forehead surrounding a nasty little cut. My mother told me how I cried and she used the cold metal of a dinner knife to hold on the cut to get the swelling to go down. It did leave a scar. I guess stitches by doctors were only gotten for serious cuts. Similarly, when my brother, Dave, got a really big wood splinter imbedded in the calf of his leg, Dad told him that he could take him to the doctor to have it taken care of, or he would give my brother five dollars if he would allow him to take the splinter out with a pair of pliers. Dave took the money. Five dollars was the doctor office fee at that time.

One time that stands out in my mind is when I was walking down the slope to the barn beside my Dad. He was on his way to milk the cows and I was singing the ABC song, and when I sang "Tell me what you think of me," Dad said, "Pretty good." I remember how great that made me feel. My Dad liked to sing and he would sing little songs to us like Oats, Peas, Beans and Barley Grow. Sometimes he might sing a song in Norwegian, I guess from his childhood. Simple things and so sweet to feel the love. I guess that there is a certain special love between a father and his daughter, just the same way I think that there is a tender love between a mother and her sons and the parents seemed to transfer this closeness in the same way to the defense of the children in a subtle, but sure, way.

Living in the country where farm homes are probably about half a mile apart, we didn't have daily contact with other children outside of our home. Of course, we went to Sunday School and worship services on Sunday, so we learned social skills there and during family visits in the homes of grandparents and aunts and uncles, a common Sunday occurrence. Other times, these same families would drop in at our house and suppers were shared. Children played games, women visited and shared recipes and news of the family and the neighborhood, while men discussed crops and politics.

When I was a little older, maybe about five, I was allowed to cut across a pasture to the farmhouse of a neighbor. This had been prearranged by the mothers, and I'm sure I was being monitored at a distance as I braved going through the pasture with big cows grazing and watching my movements. Cows have a way of trying to be friends with humans. Cows seem to enjoy the company of people, perhaps because they know that their welfare depends on the care given to them by us. In addition, domesticated animals have an enormous curiosity about any moving object and like to get up close where they can check it out. They are accustomed to heeding the call to come home in the afternoons to be milked and fed at the barn. To a little girl they were big and maybe didn't seem quite so friendly. I seem to recall spending the afternoon playing with my friend, but also dreading the long walk back home through the herd of cows. Of course, I made it without any harm, but I learned a huge lesson in humility.

We always had a vegetable garden where my mother would tend to the weeding and picking for fresh eating in season and for canning to be consumed during the winter months. There was a wide range of food including potatoes, carrots, beans, onions, beets, and, of course, a big sweet corn patch. It was always called the garden until World War II, when it got a name. Everyone was asked by the president to have a Victory Garden. I remember being out in the garden with some of the family, maybe my Dad and brothers, just before the sun went down in the fall, getting the last of the carrots out of the ground and the talk was of the Victory Garden and what that meant.

Of all of the things that went on during those times, I distinctly remember the rationing. Although we lived on a farm and owned milk cows, certain things like butter were rationed. The milk truck from the local creamery would pick up the milk and drop off the butter for us. However, we still had to have the ration stamps to give to the driver for the butter that he left us. I can still picture the closet in my parents' bedroom and at least one time being sent to the closet to bring my mothers' purse to her so that she could get the ration stamps out to give to the truck driver. I clearly remember the handbag as a striped brocade clutch with a gold clasp. It's one of those images that became stuck in my head.

There was always the tradition of placing flowers on the graves of our family members before the Memorial Day Parade. This was a big deal back then. Flowers were picked or bought and laid on the graves of our grandparents and our baby sister the day before Memorial Day. In my earliest remembrances I remember hoping that the lilac bush would bloom in time to be used as bouquets for the cemetery. These and other flowers in bloom would decorate the graves. Later, it became customary to order flowers from the local florist. Did they mean as much, I wonder? That was when Memorial Day was observed on May thirtieth, not necessarily on a Monday. We grew up calling this day Decoration Day. Sometime after World War II the name of the holiday was changed to Memorial Day and now honors all United States veterans of all wars. There was a parade that started at the National Guard Armory and that marched out to the cemetery on the edge of town. Anyone who was a member of the high school band, Campfire Girls or Boy Scouts would march in the parade. Of course, there were veterans of wars who put on their old uniforms and walked in the parade. It could be compared to the Fourth of July celebrations here in the South. At the conclusion of the parade would be a ceremony at the military memorial in the middle of the cemetery including the gun salutes. Afterwards the crowd would disburse to visit the graves of all of the friends and relatives who had passed. There might have been a family picnic, a kind of small family reunion later or we may have returned home to go about our lives. School would be out for the year by Memorial Day so our summer had begun!

On Sundays the family would attend Sunday School and morning church services. The church we attended when I was born, and for the next five years, was three miles or so from our house. In the warm months of summer we would often go to the little village general store where Dad would buy the Sunday edition of the Minneapolis Star and Tribune and as a special treat sometimes, some ice cream for dessert. My dad used to read some of the comic strips to me in the afternoon. I still feel myself snuggling up to him on the sofa for that special time. When I was born, the pastor of the Lutheran church we went to was away for some reason. Maybe it was a vacation or a sabbatical, but, for whatever reason, the pastor in the church in town was asked to perform the baptismal rites in our home. Five years later, when we actually moved membership to the church in town, my parents were surprised to learn that I was already a member of that church. I didn't get to stand up with the rest of the family to be accepted into the new congregation.

In those years during the time of rationing I remember churning butter in a big tall can with wooden paddles on the end of a stick. As Mom or Dad would work the stick up and down, the paddles inside the can would turn and, eventually we would have butter and buttermilk. I don't know if this was to supplement the butter we bought for which we had ration stamps or exactly what the circumstances were. Some things such as these grown-up problems and were not discussed with the children around. Of course we came to understand that we didn't drive the car unnecessarily in those years of the war because of the inability to get new tires and the shortage of gas, which was also rationed. I vaguely recall the drives to collect old tires and scrap metal. Since there wasn't a family that didn't have someone in the military at that time, everyone was involved in the war effort. These were willing sacrifices everyone made with the hope that the war would soon end.

World War II was what I knew when I learned to walk and talk and meet my brothers and parents, grandparents, aunts, uncles, cousins and learn their names. During the carefree, happy, early days of my life I knew there was war, even though I had no concept of what that meant until later. I had two cousins who were close to my family who were in the war; Russell in Europe, and Arnold in the Philippines. I wrote letters to my cousin Arnold who was stationed in the Pacific. I was too little to know how to spell many words, but I knew my letters and my mother would spell out the words for me as I wrote on air mail stationery and waited to get a letter back from him. When he finally came home to his fiancée, I was a flower girl in his wedding. He brought a gift for me, a bracelet that he had made from a piece of an airplane wing, a flower etched into the surface.

Here is a letter Arnold, an army medic, had written to Russell and shared with us by Russell's son.

Philippine Islands
Jan.12, 1945

Dear Russ,

Just got to thinking that it is a shame that I have waited so long in writing to you. I guess you realize Russ that during war a fella does not always get to do the things he likes to do. Of course, Russ, I know there have been times that I could have put in a few minutes if I had watched my time a little more, so I guess I'll have to call it neglect. Of course, when the bullets were flying it seemed that a person didn't think much about writing or anything else. I don't know if you have had such an

experience yet or not, but I have, Russ, and I know just how uncomfort-
able it can be.

The hottest spot I ever was in was on the last place I was. A Jap shot
at me when I was working on a buddy, so I jumped behind a big coconut
tree as that was the only place I could think of in a hurry and he knew
I was back there so he kept shooting at the trunk of the tree and every
time he hit it I could feel it in the tree. So I laid there as still as I could
looking past the side of the tree now and then to see if I could spot him as
I had my little carbine rifle ready if I had seen him. I would have used a
whole clip on him but couldn't see him. But some of the boys ahead of me
finally spotted him in the top of a coconut tree (and did they ever fill him
full). Yes, that's one yellow belly that won't do any more sniping. I could
go on all day, Russ, telling you of different times, but I'd rather not.

Now promise me, Russ, please don't mention what I told you to your
folks or anyone. You see, if they should happen to talk to someone about
it, why it could come back to my folks and I wouldn't want them to
know anything about all such stuff. They would only worry, you see, so
keep it to yourself, Russ.

I'll try to write more often hereafter.
Goodnite Russ

As ever,
Arnold

A letter written to his aunt, my mother, four months before the
letter to Russell does not reveal the anxiety shown in the later correspondence. Maybe Arnold just didn't want his true feelings to be
known to his parents and their generation. Arnold seemed to be a
very sensitive person and was always mindful of his parents' concern
for him. Here, then, is a more calm story written from the Pacific by
Arnold:

New Guinea
September 19, 1944

Dear Folks,
Saturday night so guess I'll do a little writing. I realize my letters are
not very interesting as we cannot write about the different things that

would make up an interesting letter, so about all it amounts to I guess is just to let you know I'm all well and getting along very nicely. Thank God for that.

Tomorrow I plan to attend church services if we have any. As a rule they're pretty regular about having them. We have a very fine chaplain. He sure is a good speaker.

I'm glad Hannah is feeling better now. You see, if someone is sick back there, it worries me a great deal. In fact, I'd rather not know about it. It's just a natural tendency I guess that we all have when it comes to that. If everything's ok back there if seems to go along better over here, too. See what I mean.

Suppose the boys have grown up now so they're able to do most any-thing around the farm now, huh: I'll bet I won't hardly know some of the kids back around there when I get back. That and many other changes that have taken place during my absence. But, I suppose Olaf hasn't lost any weight or changed much. Just as husky as ever. Tell him I'll take him on a few rounds when I get back! It's for sure I'd have my hands full, but then I can run pretty fast, you know. Ha! Ha!

We go swimming quite often in the beach and it's loads of fun only I don't care much for salt water. We have a nice stream that runs down from the mountains that's really perfect. It's five foot deep in places and we can see the bottom clear as day. The water is quite cold but I like that especially when it's a hot day.

Well, be sure to tell me all about yourself next time you write. I'll drop Clarence a letter soon. Tell him that. Goodnight and may God bless you.

As ever,
Arnold

To the younger generation his experiences seemed exciting and I am sure we were assured of our cousins' bravery and that it was only a matter of time before both Arnold and Russell would be returned to us and to their homes. After Arnold came home and married, I remember hearing of Arnold's nightmares of the war for some time. He and many others had to fight this war over and over, ducking or flattening themselves on the ground or floor at the sound of a sudden noise, such as a clap of thunder.

The Lean Years

Going from Little Sister to Big Sister

꩜

Thankfully, most of us are not aware of family circumstances when we are small children. We were happy and had plenty of food to eat, and, best of all, had loving parents who didn't let us know that they were struggling to make things better for all of us. Only after growing up did we realize that we didn't have as big a Christmas as a lot of other people and not everyone had to wear hand-me-downs from older cousins. Sometimes we had patches on patches on our play clothes, but there were no embarrassing holes in them. These were the years when my parents were saving as much as possible with a goal of purchasing a bigger, more profitable farm.

So it was just before my 6th birthday when the family moved from the rental farm to a small farm about 20 miles away. This was my parents first farm that they owned and, though it was not that big and the farm house and buildings not that beautiful, I understand now that owning his own farm was a matter of pride for my father for he was a hard working, ambitious person. Also, I'm sure that a large portion of the revenue from the rental farm went to the land owner. We were fortunate to have lived on this little farm during some dry years, and so the farm did pretty well and my parents were able to buy a bigger and better farm after that. After we had left, there were some rainier than usual years and much of this farm lay under water when the nearby river overflowed its banks.

The little farm had some great things about it. It had a large apple orchard that we profited from year round. We ate fresh apples and Mom made apple pies in the summer. In the late summer and early fall she made apple sauce, apple butter and used apples every other way she knew to preserve them. The little crab apples made the best

15

apple jelly and the big, red apples were so delicious. All of the children attending our school stopped by after school to grab apples to eat.

The county school where I began the first grade and stayed until the third grade was across the road from our house. We could run to school in a minute. This was known as District #25 school in Lac qui Parle County. We usually came home for lunch unless the weather was really bad, when we would take a lunch box or a brown bag with us. This school was a lot larger than a lot of the other country schools around. It even had indoor restrooms and a separate room for library books. This was a one-room school with one teacher teaching eight grades. The children were arranged by grades in rows. The teacher sat at the front and viewed the first graders to her right and other grades in groups, ending with the eighth grade students sitting on her far left. How much better can it get when you have two older brothers in the same room with you to protect you when you go to school for the first time? I felt that they were proud of what I had learned from them at home before I was privileged to start school, but I also soon realized that it was my responsibility to make them proud of me. "Why did you stop counting when you got to one hundred?" was the first thing that they said to me after the first day of school.

By the way, since there was no such thing as kindergarten or preschool at the time, our early progress in school was in some ways dependent upon what we had learned at home prior to starting school. My oldest brother, Roger, who had been coached at home, I'm sure, by my mother, was promoted from the 1st grade to the 3rd grade. As a result, he was able to graduate from high school a few days before his 17th birthday. My youngest brother, Paul, was allowed to enter 1st grade at the age of 5 1/2. (Perhaps we could all have been home schooled if that had been a possibility at the time.)

There were probably around twenty-five kids in the school. Each grade had three-to-five students. The teacher would get everyone started on an assignment and then spend probably fifteen minutes or so with each individual class. We would have a fifteen-minute recess in the morning and in the afternoon and a half-hour lunch break at noon. School started at nine o'clock and was out at four in the afternoon. We had the usual parties for Halloween, Thanksgiving, Christmas and Valentine's Day. Then there was the 'play day' in the spring when several schools in the surrounding area would all come together at one of the schools and play games and compete in outdoor activities. Come to think of it, we must have had a lot of fun! This was an event at all of the county schools.

We were a diverse community. Some families probably had more than others, and one family I remember in particular had very little. This was a family of four boys and I can't imagine how they managed to survive. They came to school, often unwashed and disheveled. They were pretty rough-and-tumble. They were all older than I, thankfully, but even as a first-grader I noticed they were unkempt. My older brothers rode bikes to the house where the four boys lived, I guess on a Saturday or maybe on a day during the summer. They came home to report that when they came up to the house, chickens flew out of the windows in the house. My brothers didn't stay long, I don't believe. Nor did the family stay in the neighborhood very long. What I assume was that they couldn't pay the rent, although I don't know that for a fact. They were reclusive and no one learned much more than their names. As I remember, one of the boys was mentally retarded and never learned anything. I remember that his name was Glenn. Later, we heard that he had gotten polio and died. Sad, sad, sad. There were also families living in the neighborhood who I considered more well off than my family. I concluded this when one of the girls in one of the families had a new teddy bear coat. This was a tan colored coat, made of a fuzzy velour type material. I thought that this imitation fur coat was the most luxurious thing I had ever seen!

Being a little sister, I didn't realize that being proud of my brothers coming out on top in playground fights did not allow me the luxury of telling about it to Mom and Dad when we got home from school. How was I to know that they weren't supposed to fight? They heard about it from Mom and Dad and I, in turn, was scolded for telling by my brothers. This was just one more lesson I learned growing up. I remember when the weather was really cold, we would play games in the basement of the school. It may seem strange that there was a basement. It had a concrete floor and was simply one big room, but it helped to keep the classroom warm. The boys in school would play hockey in the basement, using brooms and mop handles for hockey sticks. I got too close to the sharp end of the mop handle that my oldest brother was wielding and to this day have a scar on my cheek as a result.

The war finally ended when we lived on that little farm after a beloved and respected president died. Things began to return to normal, so I heard. This was the only life I knew about. But everyone seemed so happy and relieved to go about their business without rationing. Families were overjoyed to have their loved ones home from the war overseas. Again, life was good as a little girl growing up in the farmlands in Minnesota.

At some time during World War II, my cousin Harriet met and married Rex, a member of the RAF whom she met when he was on leave and stationed in Canada. They were visiting Harriet's parents and came to dinner one evening during a visit from their home in England. I can remember as a child of probably five years of age, being fascinated by Rex's British accent, specifically remarking "and bananas, too." Shortages were even greater in England than we experienced and we learned that there was more than one way to pronounce bah-nah-na! Harriet and Rex lived in England until the end of the war when they moved to Minneapolis with their little daughter, Susan, whose British accent was even more appealing. Rex was a photographer who worked at the University of Minnesota children's hospital for many years.

My younger brother was named Paul and he became my buddy, since, until he got a little older, he would hang around with me and if I was playing girl things he didn't mind being my baby or my husband or whatever fit into my imagination at any particular time. Only when he got a little older did he take up cowboy and superhero games. He got pretty good at helping me make mud cakes and pies before he got too old for the sissy stuff. But, before Paul joined me I was pretty good at entertaining myself. The corn crib held corn on the cob and there was a hand corn shucker (I think that we actually called it a "sheller") that we used to get the corn off of the cobs for the chickens. This was fun stuff. Maybe the thrill of it was simply doing something new.

My brothers seemed to be good to me most of the time. When their friends came around I wasn't needed and was reminded that I was a girl and should go to the house to be with Mom. That hurt my feelings, but I didn't want to stay around to be ridiculed by stupid boys, so I would leave. They were nice to me at other times. I remember the time they fixed the broken slats in my doll crib. How the slats got broken in the first place remains a mystery to me. There were pine trees planted on one side of the house in two rows that formed perfect squares in between them. This was perfect for playhouse rooms. My genius older brothers made furniture for the playhouse. Stumps made perfect chairs. Some even had a board nailed to the stump so the chairs could have a back on them. Mom used to buy fruit like pears and cherries to preserve for the winter. The crates the fruit came in made lovely cupboards for the playhouse. They were simply nailed to the trees and I put Aunt Laura's old discarded cups and saucers on the shelves. Aunt Laura always found uses for things she no longer wanted. Paul and I had a lot of fun out there, as long as it didn't get too boring for Paul.

Finally, I was presented with a baby sister when I was five years old. She was named Lois, but I hardly had time to get used to her when Mom had a ruptured appendix during her sixth pregnancy. We were sent to school that morning and saw the ambulance go by on the road, taking my mother to the hospital. Later, we found out that a new sister, Marian, had been born but had died shortly after birth. In those days, there weren't any intensive care units for preemies in the small town hospitals and she never had a chance. Mom was sick for a long time following her surgery and Paul, little Lois and I were sent to stay with relatives until things got sorted out. Much later, when our lives got back to normal, we were told that our mother had nearly died.

Lois was sent to stay with Mom's brother, Rob, our World War I hero and his wife, Aunt Laura. She ended up staying there for quite some time and they became extremely fond of her. Their only son, Russell, was in the army in Europe, and a toddler in the house was more than likely a welcome distraction to them. I think that they would have gladly adopted her if they had been allowed. Paul stayed with Aunt Nora and her husband, Johnny, for some time. Ironically, Nora was the sister who served as substitute mother to Mom when she was little.

I went to stay with Grandma and Grandpa, my dad's parents, who had retired from farming and who were now living in the neighboring town. It was summertime and the little girl who lived down the block from them was about my age. She brought her playing cards with her and came to play with me. She had real playing cards, not Old Maid cards, and taught me how to play Gin Rummy and Crazy Eights. Big mistake! I was catching on and getting pretty good at these new card games. We were sitting on the floor on Grandma and Grandpa's front porch when my sweet, gentle, soft-spoken Grandma found us playing with the devil's toys. My new friend was sent home with her cards and I was told in no uncertain words that this was bad. I had to listen real close to what Grandma said to understand her through the Norwegian brogue, but I was able to figure out in a hurry that playing cards was a sin and would not be allowed in her house. Things sort of took a downhill turn after that. I was lonesome and homesick. Aunt Clara, Dad's sister was a nurse and was working in the hospital or nursing home at the time and was living with Grandma and Grandpa. There were only two bedrooms in the little house, so I shared bed and bedroom with Aunt Clara for the time I stayed there. I do remember a floral scent that came with Aunt Clara. She must have kept the cologne bottle secret from me since I never saw where the smell originated. I can still imagine the scent to this day.

Living in a house for two weeks with three adults for company was a far cry from what I had been used to at home. Things were so quiet. Aunt Clara had already left for work when I got up, I guess, since I don't remember seeing her at breakfast. Before breakfast, Grandpa would reach over to the window sill by the breakfast table for his Bible written in the Norwegian language. He would read a few verses, none of which I could understand, since I only knew a few Norwegian words, but I can still see the soft smile on Grandma's face as he read. After breakfast, Grandpa would go outside to work in his little garden along the fence. It wasn't big, but my, was it neat and clean? He would weed and water the garden and then clip and trim the other plants in the yard. I remember the prettiest rose and peony bushes. They had a lawn that showed a proud homeowner.

In the meantime, Grandma would wash the breakfast dishes

and then came the painful procedure of combing out my long hair and making new braids. Every hair had to be smoothed to my head, even if it took a little Vaseline to keep it in place. I remember that Grandma said she couldn't braid my hair like my mother, who did the French braid, but I must have had the tightest, neatest braids in town! Grandma's hair was long, down to her waist, and if I got up early enough, I could see her combing her hair, then braiding it into one long braid and putting it up on the back of her head. Dear Grandma, always the same, always neat, always wearing the long dresses that came down to just above the ankle and the practical shoes, some black, some white.

We all felt bad and perhaps neglected while Mom was going through her recovery. We had help for a time keeping us in clean clothes and preparing hot meals for us. This was not an automated house by any stretch. As a matter of fact, the house was so small that there wasn't room for a washing machine. The first addition, as I recall, when we moved into the house was a small, white frame, windowless shed in the back yard. As a matter of fact, if I remember correctly, this shed was actually a shed that was made to serve as a brooder house for chicks. When we moved to our next farm this shed came with us and it was to this little building that Dad would deliver the baby chickens from the hatchery, there to be raised into laying hens. But, at first, this was the wash house, where my mother had her wringer washing machine and galvanized rinse tubs. Water had to be carried to the wash house in pails, I guess by my dad, on wash day. I think that there was a two burner kerosene heater for heating the water. Clothes were then washed, rinsed and carried out to the clothesline to dry, winter and summer. In the cold winter, clothes were brought in freeze dried and finished drying on wooden racks, wherever there was room. These racks were made so that they would fold flat when not in use.

Room was sparse in the house. The rooms were small and few. Two rooms upstairs, boys on the left and girls on the right. Two beds for three boys and one bed for two girls. The entire house was heated with a kerosene heater in the living room. As a result, there was very little heat in the bedrooms upstairs. The baby, first Paul, then Lois, slept in the crib in the dining room for a couple of years. The 'master' bedroom was too small for the crib. So, we would get our pajamas on before running up to our beds to get under the flannel sheets and quilts. Baby sisters give off a lot of heat, but it didn't take long to realize that the warmest heat generated from a baby is not only warm, but also wet.

I remember the kitchen as being very small. There was just room for a table and chairs on one end and one wall had cabinets and a sink with a pump for water from the cistern. Water for drinking had to be brought in from the well outside. Of course, there was the big old wood burning cook stove, green in color. It made the most wonderful loaves of bread and served as an additional heat source in the winter (as well as in the summer!). The reservoir at one end of the stove held hot water for all the household needs, including dish washing and baths. Farmhouses that were built in the early 20th century did not come with a bathroom or running water. Baths would be taken in the kitchen in a portable tub. As a matter of fact, one of the tubs from the washhouse doubled as a tub for bathing. It took a certain amount of engineering skill to regulate the temperature of the stove top and the oven to be able to cook and bake. The front of the oven door displayed a temperature gauge that supposedly was very accurate, but I remember a few years later at the next home, my mother asked for and got a new electric stove which made the cook's life easier with the temperature selections available. But, even Mom said the old wood-burning stove made the best bread!

When the brothers were not entertaining friends, sisters were okay to have around to play "Cops and Robbers," "Cowboys and Indians" and activities that were better with larger numbers. That was when I learned how to make rubber guns out of scrap lumber and old rubber inner tubes. I could even make a bow from tender branches and twine and with arrows carved from wood roofing shingles and I became a pretty good Indian. Dad was pretty tolerant of our using his tools and work shed to make our own toys. He tried to impress on us the need to return tools to the spot that they came from and not to waste things like nails. Things like cap guns and BB guns didn't come easy at that time of our lives. We used wood scraps to make wooden boats to float in the stock tank in the barnyard, too. Most of the time we didn't care that they didn't get painted. It was just a smaller piece

of wood nailed to a larger piece of wood with the one end pointed
to form the bow of the boat. A nail would be pounded into the front
end of the boat. With a piece of twine or string tied to it, we were
able to steer it around in the stock tank in the barnyard. We spent as
much time building as we did playing with the things we built, probably. We were just a bunch of little do-it-yourselfers.

The times I spent in the garage at the workbench growing up
gave me the courage to handle a vise, hammer, screwdriver, and saw
and later the ability to use power saws and other guy stuff. I can hang
pictures and put up a towel rack. I put bookshelves and desk chairs
together without hesitation. I learned how to replace a plug on a lamp
by watching Dad do that with a toaster. Most people don't keep their
small appliances long enough today to need to know how to do these
things, but I learned not to be afraid of electricity from an early age.
I have replaced wall outlets and if necessary will shut the breaker off
to be able to do these things, being respectful of all things bigger than
me. Give me enough time and I can and will do a lot of things some
women wouldn't think of attempting.

HAPPY TIMES
Through the Eyes of a Child

Today I hear about young adolescents getting into trouble, often, they say, because of the lack of supervision. I wonder how these same kids might get along on a farm, as did my siblings and I. We knew our Mom and Dad were not far away, but we spent an awful lot of time playing by our own rules and sometimes getting into trouble, or we came really close to being in trouble or getting hurt. You know, children don't always have a lot of common sense when adventure strikes. We knew we weren't allowed to crawl up onto hay stacks or straw bales, because of the danger of the stacks coming down on us and suffocating us. One of the fears of my mother was our playing in the bin of flax seed in the granary. We discovered that the coolest place to be on a hot summer day was laying in the flax bin. Flax seed is very small and so very smooth and silky to the touch. Explaining to us how we could smother ourselves by sinking into the grain and seeing how it frightened our mother to know we were near to that side of the granary taught us to stay out of there. Parents who raised their children on a farm knew of the dangers around us and tried to warn us, but some activities are so tempting—and don't all young people think that they are indestructible?

One example of young exuberance could be found by watching my brother, Dave, tempting fate many times. My mother liked to say that he was accident prone, and that my be true up to a point, but it seems as though he was just trying to do as many things as he had time to do. Why else would he climb up to the top of the seventy-five

25

foot windmill and sit on the narrow platform next to the blades and
try to see if he could see South Dakota from there? He more than
likely saw South Dakota from that height. We weren't that far from
the state line. He was the one always jumping off the roof of the old
brooder house or was seeing how high he could get up into a tree.
He tried daredevil tricks on the horse. On the other hand, he quite
innocently was bitten by a neighbors' dog who didn't like the bicycle
coming into their yard. He had to have stitches in the calf of his leg
on that occasion.

Most of our days were, in fact, relatively quiet. When there was
the occasional moment of excitement, it was usually unexpected and
unwanted. I refer, in particular, to the day that Dad took my little
sister, Lois, by the hand to allow her to go down to the barn with
him while he did the morning chores. It was in the early spring and
the rest of us were in school. Mom may have been trying to get the
laundry done that morning and was happy to have Dad look after my
three or four year old sister. We had only recently moved to this farm
and the previous owners asked to leave their dog with us. Since we
didn't have a dog at this time, we adopted him. The only problem was
that this dog had never been around children before, and although we
knew he wasn't very friendly, we didn't really fear him. Dad and Lois
stopped at the windmill on the way to the barn. It was time to shut
the water off that ran to the water tank in the barn. Dad dropped
Lois' hand for the brief moment it would take to turn off the water,
and in that split second, the dog attacked Lois and nailed her to the
ground. Luckily, it was cold and Lois was wearing a snowsuit with
attached hood. The dog had his mouth around her throat when Dad
turned around to see him standing over her. Dad quickly picked Lois
up and took her back to the house, where he grabbed his gun, and
returned to kill the dog where he stood. I had not known my Dad to
react with such fierce anger. I can only imagine how he must have felt
that day. I still can see the little blue snowsuit with a little red trim
that Lois wore. Could Mom have held up the snowsuit to show us
and emphasize how thankful we should all be that she was wearing
protection around her neck and having her protector, Dad, so close to
her? I'm sure that we would have told of the excitement concerning
our baby sister and the mad dog at school the next day. I'm sure we

must have been bursting with pride in our Dad and his heroic deed! Our new schoolmates probably thought we would bring some excitement into their lives as well. Certainly the addition of our family to the school district enabled the school to run for a few more years, until the number of students dwindled down to six, making it inadvisable to keep the school open.

The short days of winter gave us more time after dark to spend with homework and quiet indoor activities. Mom had a teacher's activity book that we referred to many times on cold days. I wish I had that book now to help me to remember the projects we took from it. It demonstrated how to cut out snowflakes from folded sheets of paper and how to make valentines from red construction paper and paper doilies. I remember making boxes from paper, folded and glued. (The glue we often used was actually a paste we made from flour and water.) There was the inevitable jigsaw puzzle. Mom loved putting the puzzles together and we quickly jumped into the fun. I don't think the boys got much satisfaction from jig saw puzzles, but Paul would saunter by, and when no one was looking, would grab one or two puzzle pieces and come back just in time to lay in the last piece.

Long before we had television, we had the radio. The first one I remember was a big console model that was relegated to a corner in the dining room. When we ate our three meals a day we were in the kitchen, so until we got a table model radio that found its home on the kitchen counter, we ate with only the table conversations heard in the house. I still remember crowding around the big radio after supper to hear the evening broadcasts of the news and later the stories of The Shadow, The FBI in Peace and War, Inner Sanctum and music programming. In the mornings the radio brought us the overnight breaking news. My mother would listen to The Arthur Godfrey show. After the noonday meal, which was referred to as dinner, we could hear the noonday news including the farm market report. Then my dad would read the mail and the newspaper. Soap operas accompanied my mother in the afternoons as she did the ironing and baking. I remember her listening to The Romance of Helen Trent and The Guiding Light. Sunday morning before we all got up, Mom would be listening to gospel music. In the evenings we heard the evening news with Walter Cronkite. We didn't know that we would rather have had television until we finally got our first black-and-white TV that had poor reception on all of the two channels. I remember that the first television set I saw in a home was owned by Aunt Nora and Uncle Johnny. It should probably have been a deterrent to anyone else eager to own their own set based on the quality of the picture. But, the excitement of television was epidemic. Everyone had to have one. Maybe seeing Aunt Nora with her eyes glued to her TV every afternoon watching baseball convinced others that this was great entertainment. Television had found a prominent place in our living room and the family could watch American Bandstand, Red Skelton and The Honeymooners together. The images on the television in the early days were poor and fuzzy at best. Program options, especially in the rural areas, were few, so there was little or no discussion over what channel we would watch and there was certainly nothing offered to us that was offensive even to the most discerning parents.

Before television, we were able to go the local movie theatre and see movies that had been around a few times before they came to us. The Saturday matinees brought us westerns and sometimes we could stay for a double feature. Saturday night was a favorite night for my parents to go visiting with aunts and uncles. That usually meant that we could go to see the movie showing at the theatre. Nobody had to worry about the movie being too mature or risqué for us to see. Those movies didn't make it to the theatre, if there were any. Before the times of television, news reels were shown on the neighborhood movie screens. I remember during the war (World War II) we saw news videos from the battlefields. This made the war more real to us. We saw the bombed out buildings in France and England and the faces of the soldiers on the ground as well as planes flying over the war zone, firing at enemy planes. We had to admire the bravery of the reporters as well as the fighting men as they were all exposed to enemy attacks. Then the mood was lifted with the cartoons shown before all of the movies. Of course, before the main feature began we were shown the previews of coming attractions. There were usually three different movies played during the week. When the movie was over we would walk to the house of the relatives that Mom and Dad were visiting. That was probably a maximum of ten blocks to walk and, unless it was in the wintertime when we could feel the Minnesota cold, it wasn't bad at all. There was always a plate of cookies or a piece of cake for us when we got there. I remember at that time the cost of the movie was nine cents, so with fifteen cents we could get a bag of popcorn and a penny candy such as Mary Jane's and Tootsie Rolls to eat during the movie.

I attended elementary school in two different schools. I was in the third grade when we moved to the second one, District 7, and this time the school was smaller than the first one. It had a cloakroom entry and a one-room classroom for eight grades. The building had a basement, so in the wintertime, if it was very cold, we would spend our recesses and lunch breaks playing games in the basement. I recall we played "Red Rover" and "Simon Says." This didn't mean we didn't get outside during the day. The boys' and girls' outhouses were a short walk from the school. When it was cold, nobody chose to stay away from the classroom very long on a bathroom break. One thing comes to mind when I think of the times we spent in the basement. We took turns (or maybe it was a punishment for bad behavior) sweeping the floor in the basement. We used sweeping compound to keep the dust from flying into the air. I wonder if the same green compound is still used. Hmmm.

Our house was about a quarter of a mile from school, shorter if we cut across the field. That's what we usually did during the winter when the snow was frozen on the field and walking was pretty easy, unless we came across a big snowdrift and went through the crust, filling our boots with snow. Sometimes we were unlucky enough to lose our balance when we dropped through, and would fill our mittens with snow, drop our lunch boxes and whatever else we were taking to school that day. Oh, yeah, winters in Minnesota are nothing but fun. There is something sinister about telling kids how much fun they are having while they feel as though they are frozen while playing in the snow, encumbered with heavy snowsuits and trying to be athletic with a scarf over the nose and mouth. As we would sled, ski, play ice hockey, build snow forts, hit each other with snow balls and make snow angels, we would always get snow into our boots and mittens and usually down our neck. Some kids enjoy that kind of torture, but I finally realized that I didn't have to spend nine months out of the year enjoying snow and ice, slippery roads and sidewalks and the other cold weather-related inconveniences. The weather wasn't going to change just for me, but I could move and find a warmer climate.

I much preferred summertime in the Midwest. There were some hot and humid days, but most times summer granted us the experience of going about barefoot, wearing shorts, and having picnics, family reunions and taking trips down to the river for the afternoon. There we would fish for bullheads, ugly fish that remind me of catfish to look at them. Get back before the sun went down, though, or mosquitoes would be sure to try to take half of the blood from your bare arms and legs. Very few people had air conditioning then and there were some pretty hot nights in the middle of summer and therefore it was hard to get to sleep until closer to daybreak. This meant that sometimes we were allowed to sleep on pallets on the living room floor or on the front porch. The upstairs bedrooms just wouldn't be cool enough on a still and humid night. Mom would help by finding some worn quilts to lay on the floor. We would bring our pillows and sheets from our beds. When we awoke we could be found under the covers with a morning breeze coming in through the windows. This would be even more fun if a cousin or two were spending the night. Then it could be called a big pajama party. Sleeping outdoors could have been a great option were it not for the Minnesota "state bird," the mosquito!

School always began on the Tuesday after Labor Day, and in preparation we looked forward to a new outfit to wear on the first day of school in the fall and along with that we looked forward to a new pencil box and tablet or notebooks. Really special pencil boxes came with a six-inch ruler and maybe a protractor. Ah, the smell of a new pencil being sharpened and the aroma of Crayolas when a new box is opened. As if that were not enough, sometimes there was a new teacher. I remember the visits from the county school superintendent, Mr. Wrooley. Apparently, the teacher may have been given a short advance notice of his visits and would caution all of us to be on our best behavior when he made his appearance. I'm sure the teacher was much more nervous than any of the students were, as Mr. Wrooley would take a seat in the back of the schoolroom and observed us doing our school work and sitting in class. Near the end of his visit the students were released for recess while teacher and superintendent had a conversation. My sister reminds me that she and some of her friends would creep outside to crouch under the open window in an attempt to hear what they were talking about. Could they actually understand anything that was being said? Of course not. Consider the consequences had they been caught at the dastardly deed!

Along with the beginning of a new school year, fall brought with it cooler days, an abundance of apples from the orchard, leaves changing colors and crisp evenings. Saturdays sometimes included listening to football games in the afternoon. I didn't realize that my mother had much interest in the game until I saw her in the kitchen, baking for the weekend and listening to the Minnesota Gophers game on the radio. The last hay crop would be brought in for storage in the hay loft in the barn and the corn and soy beans would be harvested before the fall rains, which would ruin the crops in the field. Soon we would be counting the weeks and days to Thanksgiving and we would wonder when we might see the first frost and then the first snow.

As Christmas grew near, the excitement of getting ready for the holidays consumed us. We were busy in school, making gifts for moms and dads. Of course, there were Christmas programs in school and in church. The program at school always included one-act Christmas plays. Everyone had a part in the play and there were always two or three plays, so everyone had a chance to have a speaking part in at least one play. Older children played the parts of the adults and the younger ones were either children, or in some cases angels or elves. We sang Christmas carols and songs. My mother would accompany us on the piano. She always declared that she wasn't that great of a piano player, but nonetheless, she was the best that we had. Later, we had refreshments provided by the mothers. Santa Claus would make a visit to listen to Christmas wishes. I am not sure if this was arranged every year or not, but I do remember one year, in particular, as we anticipated the visit from Santa, my dad was seen slipping out the back door. When Santa came in a few minutes later, all the children shouted my dad's name after making the natural assumption that my dad had dressed up as Santa. Imagine our surprise when Dad walked in behind Santa! Dad had only gone out to bring Santa, a friend of his, back to the school with him.

The Christmas programs at church were always held on the

Sunday night before Christmas. The Christmas story was recited and many songs were sung. When we were probably six or seven years old, my cousin, Sally and I sang a duet. The Sunday School superintendent deemed that we were capable and talented enough to perform. I don't remember what song we sang, but it was probably "Away in a Manger" or "Oh, Little Town of Bethlehem." There was no Santa Claus there, but all the children were given little decorated boxes filled with hard candy that had a red string handle. Riding home after the service didn't feel so cold with a treat in hand. The candy boxes also contained a few nuts in the shell that we let Dad have to eat. Sunday school teachers usually had a surprise for their students. I remember receiving bookmarks or a pretty pencil or something else practical.

Mothers would spend hours baking in preparation for Christmas. There would be white cookies, cut in the shape of stars and Christmas trees, decorated with colored, sugar sprinkles on top. We would have fruit cookies in the same shapes, not to mention delicious doughnuts, fudge, and divinity candies, and of course the inevitable fruit cake. Christmas was the prime time for entertaining and being entertained. It didn't matter what was going on in the rest of the world. This was a time of much rejoicing and fun for all generations. It mattered not whether we still believed in Santa or not, gift giving and receiving was such an exciting time. School would be out for the Christmas and New Year's holidays. Christmas shopping and giftwrapping would begin in earnest. Paul, always mischievous and inquisitive, would diligently search for gifts that our parents had hidden from us. He seemed to have a sixth sense of just where to look. He must have been around 6 years old and had convinced himself that there wasn't a Santa. He proclaimed more loudly and persistently as Christmas drew near. I think he was trying to get someone to prove to him that, in fact, there was a Santa Claus. A plan was developed that year to smuggle the gifts from Santa into the back porch off the kitchen. The porch was unheated and once everyone was in for the night, the door stayed closed tight. After we had finished our huge evening meal, Mom and I had cleaned up the kitchen while everyone else gathered in the living room to wait for time to open gifts. Mom made a grand entrance into the living room and I slipped in moments later, after moving the Santa gifts from the porch onto the kitchen table. We somehow convinced Paul that he had heard a noise in the kitchen after we had all quieted down. He went to investigate. Imagine his gleeful surprise when he found gifts for everyone from Santa! That was probably the best, but also the last, of Paul's Christmases with a belief in Santa.

While we were all very young, there would be a special gathering on Christmas Eve of all of my mothers' sisters and brothers with their children and some grandchildren. Names would be drawn before Christmas by someone elected to do so. Children drew names from the children's collection, but as I recall, the adults didn't have that exchange. I do remember one Christmas, one of the cousins couldn't keep the names of my sister and me straight. As a result, I was given a really young children's gift and Lois got a puzzle book or something way beyond her age. Of course, we did the swap, but I remember thinking, "Can't they tell us apart"?

On Christmas Day all of the aunts, uncles and cousins on my dad's side of the family who lived nearby would congregate at Grandpa and Grandma's house. Grandma would cook for everybody and more gift exchanges took place. I remember, after a time, waiting for time to go home and back to the gifts we had gotten earlier. We hadn't had much time to appreciate what we had gotten at home. The morning of Christmas we went to morning church services, so we were happy to get home from the grandparents' house and play with our new toys or admire our new possessions. Our grandmother gave each of her young grandchildren two pairs of mittens for Christmas, one pretty pair for Sunday or special dress up times and the other pair for play. The ones for play were usually a practical color like gray or brown and were double knit for extra warmth. The dressy ones would match or coordinate with our dressy coats.

Until Christmas and New Year, the time fairly flew by with all of the events of fall and the holidays keeping us busy. Then came the long, cold nights and the short days of winter. We were indoors too much. We weren't pampered and kept indoors and safe, but who would want to be out in the cold wet snow for long periods of time? Even though the snow was dry when we touched it, it would melt on contact with warm skin, so if we were unfortunate enough to get snow in our boots or inside our mittens (and who wasn't?) naturally it was only a matter of a short time before we were wet and cold and no amount of wool layers would keep you warm when snow got next to your skin. One very cold Thanksgiving morning when I was perhaps 10 years old, the family was heading to the house of our aunts in Watertown, South Dakota for a dinner of duck and the trimmings. About half way there something happened to the car's heater and it felt like the outdoors in the back seat, even with a car full of people. We stopped at a filling station and filled up with whatever we needed or fixed what needed to be fixed, but not before I had developed a good case of frostbite on my toes. Those dressy little shoes were no competition for the South Dakota cold. My aunts, nurses both, put my feet into cold water when we got there and no permanent damage was done, but I shall never forget the stinging heat on my toes from the cold water!

Mom and Dad belonged to The Farmers' Union. Farm families belonged either to The Farmers Union or The Farm Bureau. I don't know how the politics differed, but I do know that that is where we had our hospital insurance. There was usually some little program for entertainment and one meeting Lois and I sang for a meeting of The Farmers Union, held in the basement meeting room of the library. I thought I was too old to stand in front of a bunch of people with my little sister to sing some silly song, but we did sing. That was the same night that one of the ladies had brought a sheet cake with white icing and chocolate sprinkles on it. One of the little boys in attendance told his mother that she needed to look at that cake, because it had mouse dirt on it. I have wondered if he really believed he was seeing mouse dirt or if he was just looking for attention!

We rode the bus to school in town when there was no longer any school in the little one room school, or in the case of the older kids, when we became old enough to transfer to junior high or high school. The bus would stop at the end of our drive, and in the wintertime when it was very cold, we had to time it just right so we wouldn't have to wait too long in the cold. I don't remember ever waiting very long, so I guess that means that Mom must have had the timing down precisely to the minute, since I remember very few times that we actually missed the bus. Lois remembers that Mom would watch

from the window to see the bus as it approached from a quarter of a
mile away. Of course, coming from a large family, the trick was to get
at least one of us out of the door and started down the driveway, so
the bus driver would see someone coming and, by the time the first
one got on the bus, the rest of us were in sight or not very far behind.

Mom didn't have much time to herself with five kids and a garden
to tend. There were very few times that we came home from school
and she wasn't there, more often than not, with the aroma of fresh
baked bread or cookies waiting for us. If we didn't feel hungry when
we got into the yard, the fresh baking smells had our appetites on
edge by the time we got to the kitchen door. I guess that the only
times Mom wasn't there when we got home was if it was the day for
Ladies' Aid or Homemaker's Club.

Dave was the practical joker in our family. He loved playing practical jokes on Mom. One afternoon, he found a nest of garter snakes
in the ditch next to the driveway on his way home from elementary
school. He thought it would be fun for Mom to find them in his
empty lunch box. The first thing Mom did when we came in from
school was to clean out the lunch boxes of waxed paper and crumbs
from our lunch boxes and wipe them out. As well as I can remember
we all carried the ordinary black metal lunchboxes. This was before
advertisers targeted kids as they do now, so we would not have had
boxes decorated with the cute Disney characters or comic book
heroes. Imagine her surprise and anger when she opened Dave's box
to find those little bitsy snakes squirming around in his empty lunch
box. That is the first and last time Mom got that kind of surprise. He
had to be Mom's favorite child to be forgiven for an act such as that!
Incidentally, Dave likes to remember that it was Paul, not he, who did
that dastardly deed. I cannot be convinced of that.

Lois, being the youngest, was Dave's target for practical jokes and
teasing. Lois has never forgotten the day that Dave took her to the
nearby cornfield so that she could hear the corn growing. With the
rustle of leaves from a slight breeze, the imagination of a child could
easily be convinced that the sound was that of the growing corn.
Another time Dave set Lois up on a branch just high enough from
the ground to seem too far to jump down. He told her that she would
have to stay in the tree until she was tall enough to get down by

herself. Even with all of the tricks he played on her gullibility, she still trusted him and followed him wherever he went on the farm.

Thinking back to unusual and memorable times, there was a winter of record-breaking snow. Our home was just three miles from the edge of town, but we were trapped in our yard by the high snow drifts filling the driveway. Ordinarily, Dad would clear the road using the scraper on the front of the tractor, but this was an extraordinary amount of snow, so the only solution was to wait for the county snow plow to have time to do the job. Dad decided to take on the elements and make the trek into town to get some supplies that were needed and to pick up the mail from the post office. I'm not sure how many days had gone by since we had been out, but we all were probably getting cabin fever by this time. Dave thinks, and most likely he's correct, that Dad was running out of cigarettes, and used other excuses to necessitate the need for his solo trip. He may also have been concerned about the welfare of other families around.

With the big snows came big adventures for children. When snow covered the hay stack out in the barnyard and created a miniature mountain, we found that we could sit on the scoop end of a big grain shovel with our hands around the handle, and coast from the top of the haystack to the bottom, and keep on going for as far as the momentum would carry us. The practice of using a shovel as a sled proved hazardous. When Lois cut her tongue from the impact of coming to a short stop, Dave looked around for a villain and chose to blame me for causing the injury to Lois. I'm not sure why it wasn't just "another accident," but he seemed to feel it was somehow my fault! For more excitement there was the occasional invitation to a toboggan party. A family who lived on a farm with a river running through and surrounded by trees and hills entertained us one time that I remember. It's astounding how fast four or five kids on a toboggan can speed down a hill, trusting the person in front to steer us around the trees and bumps and get us safely to the bottom. This was followed by the long trek back to the top of the hill. The time spent on the toboggan was in part determined by the number of times one was willing to climb back to the starting point.

Strange isn't it, how sports and games resemble life? We reach for the high places in our life, only to discover that we find ourselves in a valley when we lose the focus of our life plan. We often feel the happiness of the wonderful days we are given, but, when in our selfishness of the moment, we neglect to consider our friends and family, the pleasures and happiness we enjoy fades and we find ourselves sliding downhill. Only when we gather others with us in our joy can we attain the utmost satisfaction. We have been instructed as children to share, but as we mature, the realization comes to us that we must share our happiness, as well as our possessions, with others in order to be truly fulfilled. A few words, or an understanding smile of sympathy or approval, can work wonders in the lives of others.

THE COUNTY FAIR
Exodus from Summer to Fall

Notices in the local paper and on storefronts announcing the coming of the county fair meant that our summer vacation was over. The inevitable shorter days and cool nights could be associated with the week of the county fair. Within a few short weeks we would witness the color change of the leaves and feel the urgency of harvesting the last crops of corn and soybeans from the fields. As far back as I can remember, going to the county fair in the fall was a family event. The county fair offered a variety of things to many people. In addition to the carnival rides and games, we also celebrated the original meaning of a county fair. Members of the rural community brought the results of the year's efforts to the fair to be judged and admired. For some, it was livestock displayed proudly. For others, it was accomplishments achieved in school or in the home kitchen. For those who brought entries to the fair, it was an exciting time!

The county fair revealed Grandma's competitive side. Grandma entered her preserves, baked goods, and knitted items such as her afghans. As I recall, she always won ribbons on the things she entered. Going through the exhibit buildings was not the most exciting part of the fair for me. I was expected to make the trek with Mom before I was allowed to enjoy the rides and the other midway attractions. The midway was the area in the center of the fairgrounds containing the rides and the sideshows that were brought to us by the carnival people.

I thought it was more fun to tour the barns where the farm animals were on display. Kids who raised animals for 4-H would be there early in the morning, cleaning out the stalls or pens and washing and grooming pigs, sheep and calves. I visited this venue with friends later in the day.

There were the grandstand shows. It was here that the lucky numbers were drawn for prizes that were given away. I seem to remember an instance of sitting in the bleachers at one time, but I have no recollection of what was going on at the time. I probably was trying to be patient as I waited for the chance to get out to the rides and other excitement. My brother, Dave, entered a horse riding competition one year when he was just a little guy. I think that they needed someone to fill a slot for that age group. I know that it had not been rehearsed before that day. He was proud to leave with a yellow ribbon, which meant that he had earned third place.

In one section of the fair grounds local implement dealers showed off their display of new and innovative farm equipment. That was like window shopping for Dad. I don't know if the display influenced any purchases by my dad, but it was a place where farmers from all over the county and beyond could meet and compare ideas and experiences.

There were also some special exhibitions to draw a crowd on the midway. I remember one show in particular that was supposed to feature the getaway car belonging to the gangster, John Dillinger. Dad talked about the attraction, but I don't know if he actually paid the admission price to see it. It was of special interest because John Dillinger had terrorized cities across the Midwest. He was probably one of if not the most vicious bank robbers during the era of the depression in the 1930's.

While most kids preferred hot dogs and pop, the adults would be found at one of the food booths run by various churches or community organizations. I remember now, after growing up, being at the fair and enjoying a pancake breakfast at one of the church booths. Here people could sit down on one of the benches and enjoy a good hamburger and a cup of coffee.

There was one day during the week of the fair, when kids were admitted free or for a very small charge. That was the day when we would see more of the toddlers and elementary school kids. The

"Merry-Go-Round" and kiddy rides stayed busy all afternoon.

As we got older we were allowed to roam the grounds with friends. With a string of tickets purchased for us when we came in the gate, we decided which rides we would get on, and which of the midway games we could afford. We had a little pocket change to buy something to eat. We fed on hotdogs and cotton candy and washed the food down with a pop or lemonade. I found out the hard way that it better to ride the Tilt-a-Whirl or ferris wheel before eating those things. I believe that the county fair was the place where I first saw people with tattoos, and I decided that I didn't like the way this art was displayed.

One of the exhibit buildings held the entries from the county school children. Teachers had to decide what to send to be judged. When I was in the second grade my teacher entered me in the penmanship contest. I was surprised and pleased to win a first place ribbon. I was even more surprised to learn that my entry had been sent on to the state fair and had won first place statewide.

On the last day of the fair, on Sunday, the family would usually go to the fair to see what prizes had been awarded. By Monday the midway would be dismantled and the carnival workers and their trucks and wagons would be gone. On one of those Sundays when I was 13 or 14, I had planned to meet a friend at the fair. We would be going with our parents and would join up when we got there. The plan included wearing blue jeans that day. I was ready to leave, but was stopped by Mom and Dad at the front door. Dad told me that I would not wear blue jeans on Sunday. I could change clothes or stay home. I chose to stay home. Was I being stubborn or was I feeling the peer pressure about teenage fashion? I think maybe a whole lot of both. Could this have been my take on the female revolution?

County fairs were one of the highlights for all kids living in rural America. It provided good, healthy competition for boys, girls, and adults. The people who brought the midway shows were fascinating to the kids from the country. Little did we know that most of them were only struggling to earn a living like everyone else. They would travel across the country bringing the magic of their livelihood to the sheltered way of life, as we knew it, on the farm. We thought they were living a special adventure on the road. Perhaps if we had noticed the faces of the children in the families of these nomads we might have detected a yearning for a different and more stable form of life. As the saying goes, isn't life always greener?

THE HAY MOW

Second Floor of the Barn, or Hay Loft

The hay mow is a wonderful place for kids of all ages. It might be called the gymnasium of the farm. Although it served, first and foremost, as a huge storage place for hay for the cows and horses down below, it held much more for us.

The hay mow was the place where pregnant cats went to have their kittens. They would burrow just far enough into the mound of hay to be invisible to the eye, at first glance. This was the first place that we would look to find a new batch of kittens, although they often found more obscure hiding places. I remember finding kittens out in the granary. We would not have figured that one out had we not followed the mother cat, knowing she was heading for her litter. We had to find out how many, and what colors, the kittens were.

The hay mow was also where we played basketball in the winter. My brothers' friends loved to come out from town to play a game in the private basketball court. My brothers had a basketball hoop on the wall at the end of the barn. They would sweep the floor clean of any hay in preparation for a game. As long as they didn't knock down any bales of hay stacked in the mow or otherwise interfere with the normal operation in the barn, they were free to play as long as they liked. I do remember my Dad finding evidence of someone who had smoked a cigarette while in the barn. That was the worst possible thing that anyone could have done, considering the likelihood of a spark causing a fire. As I recall, a warning was issued, and only those who obeyed the rules would be welcomed in the future. (Even though

Dad was a cigarette smoker, we never saw him smoking in or around the barn.)

We enjoyed being in the hay mow when it was frigid outdoors. There was only one danger to be considered. In each of the 4 corners of the floor, was an opening, perhaps 3 feet square. These were designed as a convenience in pitching hay to the animals in the stalls and pens below. We were accustomed to running and playing in wide open spaces. Normally we would run until we tripped or became too tired to go on. So, it happened, one day, while chasing each other in a game of tag, perhaps, or playing hide and seek, that one of us, literally, dropped out of sight. This time Paul found himself in a pile of hay in front of the horse stalls on the first floor of the barn. This was not the only time such a thing happened, but luckily nobody was injured. It was probably a little humiliating to leave the game in that way, but it certainly afforded the rest of us a good laugh, at least after being assured that there were no broken bones. Mom was the only one that failed to see the humor in the incident. Once again, one of her children escaped with a few scratches, and the only hurt was to his feelings.

The hay mow was a wonderful place to go to daydream. In a family the size of ours, it was nice to find some space away from everyone else to do some thinking or meditate, where it was quiet. There would be the occasional animal noise, but that only provided a comforting background. Just the smell of the fresh alfalfa was an invitation to climb the stairs to the hay mow and settle down on a hay bale and appreciate the solitude. It probably would take a little while to be missed, but sooner or later, if one of us was gone for too long, we would hear our name being called, and we would be awakened from our reverie.

I had another place, during spring and summer, just on the outer side of the windbreak and out of sight from the house, where I would sit on the ground with pad and pencil to put thoughts on paper. I relished being away from the sounds and activity of the rest of the farm. There I would settle on a grassy spot under a tree, in the early morning or late afternoon. At times a dog would lay at my feet, yet more often I was alone. But, the hay mow was the grandest and safest-feeling place on the farm, particularly on a rainy day in the spring. To this day, I find peace and comfort during a thunderstorm.

THE RELUCTANT TRAVELER
Pig on the Loose

My family was a farm family. The farm was a working farm and was typical of the farms in the first part of the twentieth century. In other words, not only did we raise cash crops for sale on the market, but our farm boasted a huge barn and various other buildings whose sole purpose was shelter for the animals. The grains that we raised, as I recall, were oats, wheat, rye, soybeans, corn and sometimes flax.

Some of the grain produced was used to feed the farm animals and chickens. A nourishing feed, simply known as ground feed, was made for the animals by grinding corn and oats together and was fed to animals in measured amounts. The main source of feed for cows in the summer months was grass from the pastures. After the pastures were allowed to fallow in the fall, the cows would be fed alfalfa and silage. Picturing a cow feeding from the trough in front of her stanchion, I think, "That's a contented cow." Pigs or hogs, small pigs or grown hogs, are fed a combination of grain and manufactured hog feed. The purchased feed would have added nutrients to ensure that the animals would have a well-balanced diet. The animals that lived on our farm never suffered or went hungry.

Since one of my jobs was feeding the chickens, I am reminded of the trips that I made from the granary to bring oats to the chicken house in a five-gallon pail. Another trip was required to bring water in a pail from the well to the water feeder. Since our chickens laid eggs for resale, they also received a supplement in the form of oyster shells.

This gave the eggs a harder shell easier to handle without the danger of breaking. Gathering the eggs from the nests was the final chore in the hen house. Usually this was an easy task. We would merely reach in, pick up the egg and place it in the basket. Sometimes, however, a hen might decide to try to hatch her egg, and she would protest by pecking at the hand reaching under her belly. It's possible to hold the hen's head with one hand and grab the egg with the other hand, if you're quick.

I don't remember a time that we didn't have meat at least once a day. Of course, we raised all of the meat that we ate, except for the occasional specialty meat purchased at the butcher shop. This may have been some type of ring bologna, either the regular Polish bologna or the light colored Swedish bologna. (There were a few times when we Norwegians would condescend to ingest Swedish type foods.) Other times we might have canned salmon, usually served cold and for supper on Sunday evening in the summer time. But, most of the time we had beef, pork or chicken. There was a time or two that I remember Dad treating himself to some pickled herring that had been shipped to the butcher shop. The others in the family only watched him as he enjoyed the 'delicacy'.

If I remember correctly, a grown calf and a hog would be butchered at some time in the fall. The animal would be penned up and be given feed that would be sure to produce some tender, tasty cuts of meat. A time would be arranged with the operator of the slaughter house a couple of miles from our house to bring the live animal in to be slaughtered. I seem to remember Dad needing help from my brothers to load the animal up early in the morning to deliver the animal at the agreed on time. The slaughtered animal would be transferred to the butcher in town where the meat would be cut and packaged to the desired sizes and meat cuts requested. Before we had a home freezer, the meat would be packaged and put in a rented freezer locker at the back of the butcher shop. My mother would visit the butcher shop and retrieve from the rented locker the meats that we would be using for the next several days. At home the meats would be placed in the refrigerator/ freezer to use over the next few days.

One particular evening, we were entertained by the telling of the story of the pig that almost got away on the way to slaughter.

Dad had the hog in the 2-wheeled trailer, hitched to the back of the pickup truck, and felt that the hardest part of his work was over. When he arrived at the slaughter house, Dad discovered that his passenger was no longer in the trailer. Nothing to do but retrace his path back to the farm. He found the hog in the ditch, contentedly eating grass at the side of the road. The hog apparently didn't enjoy the ride and had jumped over the side of the trailer, unbeknownst to Dad. I don't know how the hog was recaptured, or if Dad had to garner help to get the porker into the trailer for the second time that day, but his fate had already been sealed, and we had fresh pork chops the next day. I don't need to be convinced that pigs have a larger brain than most animals.

FARM LIFE IN THE FIFTIES
The Natural Flow of the Farm

W e all take note of the seasons as they roll around. Most times we are waiting for the next season to arrive when we find ourselves tired of the current one. Too hot? Can't wait for fall to get here. Everything is drab and colorless? Just wait until spring gets here. In the meantime, we are usually stuck with the day-to-day business of living from Monday to Sunday. Our routines are sculpted by work schedules and daily chores, along with plans for holidays and vacations.

On the farm in the fifties, seasons formed the framework for what the farmer did in this, his chosen profession. The farmer worked with one eye on the weather and the other eye on the demands of the land and animals. With cows, pigs, chickens and other animals, some tasks had to be completed every day with a pretty tight schedule being followed. They all had to be fed every day. Except for the time devoted to milking the cows, they would make fewer demands on their caretaker during the summer, when they could be let into the pasture during the day. In the cold weather or when the pastures went into the dormant stage, cows had to be fed stored silage and hay. The other animals depended on the farmer to bring feed and water to them, every day, year round, without fail.

The work in the fields was determined in large part by the weather. If there happened to be a late spring, planting would be delayed and the farmer had to work longer days to get the work done. Fields had to be prepared for planting by plowing and smoothing the field.

This was followed by planting at the right time to produce a crop during the growing season. Row crops had to be cultivated to rid the field of weeds, fertilizing when necessary. All this time the farmer would find himself praying for rain and hoping that hail wouldn't fall and destroy the crops in the field.

The work day would begin early. Animal chores had to be completed before going out to the field. Usually Dad would fuel the tractor and attach the equipment the night before, so he could head out to the fields as early as possible. Dad didn't like to stop once he got started, so if his coffee and sandwich weren't ready to go when he got on the tractor, someone would bring it to him mid-morning. I always enjoyed that assignment, when I would spend alone time with Dad. I don't remember what we talked about and it really didn't matter to me. It was one of the times I spent time with my dad. In the summer time, I loved getting out of bed early in the morning just to go down to the barn while Dad milked the cows. I wonder if he knew how special he was to each and every one of us. Only occasionally would Dad come home for his morning or afternoon break, and then only if the field he was working in was close to the house. Mom always had the noon meal ready for Dad when he pulled into the yard. He was ready to eat, read or listen to the news and usually take a power nap on the floor for a few minutes. By mid afternoon Dad would need an afternoon break. If he didn't have a lunch box with him after the noon meal, another trip to the field was required or he would have to come back to the house for his coffee and sandwich. As long as there was help at home to take care of the chores in the barn, Dad would likely stay out in the field until it became too hard to see. Some days our evening meals would be a little late, but we all sat down at the table together. Very rarely was there an excuse for anyone to miss this family meal.

Another rule in the family was that there would be no working on Sunday, except to prepare meals and tend to the animals. We would go to Sunday School and church on Sunday morning and spend the remainder of the day resting and visiting. One exception might be to do our school homework. Some of our teachers didn't mind giving us homework on the weekends.

The family farm was a working farm and involved the whole

family. Mom and Dad had their separate areas of expertise and the two of them formed a united front to keep the operation running. We grew up knowing that we were all important and necessary. We were given chores to do that were age relevant. When I was nine years old my older brothers had chores to do in the barn in the morning, while it was my job to make up the four beds in the bedrooms upstairs. Mom had the bed downstairs made up before the rest of us rolled out of bed. Trying to figure out head and foot of Paul's bed was a challenge. We seemed to be one room short of having a room for each of us. Paul and Dave shared a room and double bed. Paul slept a restless sleep, tugging the covers away from Dave and ending up like a cocoon in the middle of the bed. No amount of complaining from Dave seemed to make a difference. There was a period of a year or two when we found Paul sleepwalking during the early hours of the night, sometimes ranting and raving, as he wandered from room to room. Paul spent more energy getting a night's rest than he exerted during his waking hours.

My brothers took a more active role in the farm operation during the growing and harvesting season. They worked hard then and the heavy work they did was a good workout for the football season in the fall. I helped Mom with a lot of the work in the house, including such things as ironing and running errands between the basement and other two floors. I don't ever remember being totally exhausted from the work that I did. I rather think that I may have been a little pampered, considering the workload that Mom had.

I always imagined my brothers had more exciting chores to do than I did. They had a chance to drive the tractor and fun stuff like that. One summer, Dad was short one pair of hands during haying season. He thought that I could be trusted to drive the tractor around and around the field while he and my brothers pitched the hay into the hay rack that was hitched behind the tractor. I proved that I could steer the tractor just fine, but I was a poor judge of distance when I turned the tractor too sharply and tore a plank off the side of the hay wagon. That was the end of my tractor driving. Time was wasted in the field while the hay rack was repaired.

We didn't experience any devastating disasters that I remember. There was a time or two when a hail storm damaged some of the crops, but fortunately we had insurance against such losses. If I am accurate in my memory, the insurance payment paid for the expense of replanting the damaged crops. Paying for insurance was just another necessary cost of running a family farm. All of these items were recorded in Dad's farm records, and at the end of the year, I was allowed to help Dad organize all of the income and expenses before Dad would visit the tax accountant. I enjoyed helping with that part of the business end of farming! When I was younger, I would fill out orders from the Sears and Roebuck catalog and was even allowed to use a book of counter checks from the bank in my accounting play.

Since animals were an important feature on the farm, the farmer had to be alert to any problems with all of the livestock. A good veterinarian was someone whose phone number was kept handy. Besides the regular vaccinations that the vet would administer, the vet was also on call to make emergency visits to the farm. Dr. Fleming came to the rescue when one of the cows was having a calf in the breech position. The cow and calf were both fine with the help of the veterinarian. Doc Fleming was also called when a cow became ill after swallowing some baling wire that had gotten mixed in with the hay she was fed. Most of the calls to the vet were for routine shots or other services. There was a time or two when a vet was needed and Doc Fleming was on a binge. His wife handled his calls for him and she would tell the caller that Doc would not be able to make it that day if he was in the middle of one of his binges. He never attempted to conduct his services if he was drinking, thankfully, and if there was an urgent need, his wife would suggest that another vet be called. He was an excellent vet, with a problem.

Animals Whom I Have Known
Surrounded by Friends

⌘

There is much that I can tell you about animals on the farm. We were rarely without a dog and never without a cat. Of course, living on a farm meant that we had horses, cows, pigs, chickens, and sometimes sheep. One time my brother, Dave, traded a rooster for a white rabbit. Maybe we should have known and maybe my brother knew that Annabelle Linda Belle` was pregnant when she got there and so, in no time, had a litter of the prettiest little white bunnies you ever saw. They didn't last long. I think that the dog ran faster than any of the bunnies could hop.

I guess there was an unwritten law that said all boys in our family should and would have a pony or a horse to ride. After the work horses were replaced with tractors, we still had riding horses. My brothers were even given the job of gentling a horse for someone else teaching it to neck rein and be saddled and bridled. A bit of excitement occurred one Sunday afternoon when Mom and Dad were gone. Dave was riding a horse when the horse came in contact with a barbed wire fence and cut a gash in the horse's front leg. I seem to remember that Paul and I were there and we put a tourniquet on the leg to stop the blood spurting. Apparently, an artery had been punctured, but we somehow managed to stop the bleeding. Then we applied some salve and bandaged the wound. All the time, Dave was more worried about what Dad was going to say when he got home than the immediate problem. I think that we were all afraid that the horse was going to bleed to death. That didn't happen and all we suffered was the bad memory of what might have been.

We had moved from the first farm, the rental farm, to the small farm and then to the bigger, more productive farm. We still had Captain and my sister, Lois, was still just a baby. My brother, Paul, was probably about five years old at the time and was determined to take a ride on Captain. The only hindrance seemed to be the fact that he couldn't get up onto the bare back without a boost. Lois was sitting in the stroller out in the front lawn. The tray on the stroller was exactly what Paul needed to stand on to reach the back of the pony. My mother looked out the kitchen window just in time to see Paul push the stroller (with Lois in it) under the pony and climb onto the tray and from there unto the pony. My mother dared not scream for fear of startling the pony, and could only watch as Captain, dear and gentle Captain, deftly stepped over the stroller and over Lois' head and carried his rider away. Captain knew instinctively what speed was safe for the rider. I can remember, with great clarity, Paul trying his best to get the pony to gallop for him, but the most Captain would allow was a slow trot.

Dogs were an absolute necessity. We needed a dog to warn us of any approaching person, car or truck. They were supposed to help bring the cows in from pasture, but I don't remember any of the dogs we had being much good at herding. Dogs were kids' best friends, of course. We didn't buy special food for our pets. They got the leftovers and milk spared them when the cows were milked morning and night.

Only one dog was ever allowed into the house. I like to think it was because he was such a brave little thing just for surviving. I was around 13 years old when I happened to look out from the kitchen window to see a little black dog running from the granary to the barn. He stood outside the door of the barn in the pouring down rain. I went out to open the barn door for him, a shivering, pitiful little cocker spaniel. After rubbing him down with a gunny sack, I went back to the house to bring him something to eat. Then I sat with him, petting him and trying to get him dry. When I left he was just lying there, exhausted and asleep. My Dad wasn't very hopeful that evening, when he came into the house, thinking my new found pet wouldn't make it through the night. Our refugee surprised us all, when the next morning he met us at the barn door wagging his tail. He slept by my bed after that.

Some of the dogs who adopted us found our farm during pheasant hunting season. It was the general consensus that hunters acquired a dog to take hunting, then drove off without them to go back to their homes on the concrete city streets. One dog, whom I remember in particular, and who found us, turned out to be a really good work dog. He would stand at the gate at the barnyard fence and would not allow the cows to escape. Isn't it ironic that some of these same hunters who definitely gave us a valuable farm helper also were responsible for mistaking our dogs for deer and killing them? One of our dogs was discovered lying at the edge of the woods, dead, with a bullet hole in his head.

I shall remain ever thankful for growing up on a farm. It saddens me to think that so few young people have ever spent time in a dairy barn, the old-fashioned kind, where it's not all sterile and smells like disinfectant. There I would go down the front of the stanchions talking to the Holstein cows named Annabelle, Lulabelle, Clarabelle and any other belles imaginable. There's something satisfying about being able to milk a cow. We progressed to milking machines, which were much more efficient and time saving, but it just wasn't the same. And, is there anything as pretty as a little calf with big brown eyes? How could anyone not grow to love them? The new-born calves were taken from their mothers almost the minute they were born and put into a pen in the barn for the first weeks of their lives until they could be weaned and allowed out into the herd. In the meantime, they first had to be fed milk from a pail, and that was a fun job while they were still very small. They grew quickly and didn't take long to get overly impatient and tried to get milk more quickly by butting the pail. We really had to hang on tight in order to keep the milk from spilling unto the floor.

Cats loved being in the barn with the cows, especially at milking time. If you got good at it, you could aim for the cat's mouth, and, if the cat was good at it, all they had to do was open their mouths to have some warm milk. We had cats all of the time. Sometimes we got a little over-populated with them. We had a female cat who must have outlived her nine lives. She was sure to produce five kittens twice a year, spring and fall. They came in different colors and we soon figured out that when our fat mama cat got suddenly skinny, there were kittens to be found. We learned to watch her and follow her to the nest in the hay mow. When we found them, they hadn't even opened their eyes, but she kept them sequestered until she got tired of feeding them and then would bring them out to be fed some of that warm cows' milk. Cats had their purpose on the farm, also. Only rarely were mice detected in the barn or any of the other outbuildings.

A place of honor was bestowed on a fluffy, very small kitten. When Lois was just five, and before starting school, she was invited to come to the school on picture day to have her picture taken along with the enrolled students. She brought her little gray kitten with her, and today we have the picture of her and her furry friend. Talk about the cat's meow!

Roger and David belonged to 4-H and had different projects. When they entered high school, they belonged to FFA, Future Farmers of America, and one year they raised sheep. That was fun for all of us. We watched the ewes become mothers with the cutest little lambs you could ever have seen. A ewe would usually have twins, and if you think that goat kids are cute, you need to really be around lambs for a while. Of course sheep had to have names, too. I named them from the Bible. They had names like Titus, Timothy and Bartholomew. There was one special ewe whom I called Blossom. I'm not sure how she deserved that name, but she was by far the nosiest one of the bunch. One day she dipped her nose into a bucket for a drink and quickly pulled her head out, with oil drained from the tractor, up over her black nose and into the white wool under her eyes. I laughed at her and she looked at me as if to say, "That's not funny." She remained affectionate to me in spite of it all. They may have been my brothers' money-making project, but they were my friends.

There's really nothing very lovable about chickens. They run when you come near, unless you're bringing them something to eat. If you carry a pail in your hand they will accost you, both physically and vocally, knowing that you have feed for them. We raised a new flock of chickens every spring. We would get about one hundred and fifty little yellow chicks from the hatchery and bring them up to be egg layers. That's when they are cute. But, even chickens can tear at your heartstrings. There was a poor little cripple who had a deformed neck. This deformity caused her to look up all of the time. The rest of the flock didn't like her different look and picked on her every time she came near. I would stay by her and chase the rest of the hens away so she could get a chance to get to the feeder. I named her Peck-a-poo and protected her all through the summer. When winter came, the chickens were confined to the chicken house, since chickens, poor things, didn't have enough sense all the time to get in out of the cold. I worried about Peck-a-poo having to be tormented all winter in the closed chicken house. Imagine my delight when I came home from school one day to find out that Dad had taken my pet into the barn and away from the other hens. My dad, my hero!

I don't know how old we were at the time, but, as so often happens during the harvest times on the farm, there was more work to be done than there were hours in the day. It required a lot of cooperation among family members to accomplish what needed to be done. One evening, in particular, my brother, Paul, walked home from the field and found me outside feeding and watering the chickens, which was my job at the time. He informed me that Dad had sent him home to tell me that I needed to milk the cows, and that he had other chores that he was supposed to do. Dumb me, I believed him and did as I thought I had been instructed to do. Only later did I discover that I had been duped by my little brother and that he had found some time to goof off that afternoon.

Paul—My First Best Friend
And Little Brother

Since my older brothers, Roger and David, were just 2 years apart in age, they naturally spent a great deal of time together in work and play. Their interests were similar while they were growing up. Where you saw one of them, the other was sure to be nearby. They supported each other, played together, fought against each other, defended one another, and, most importantly, they loved being together in good times and not so good times, as children, and later as adults.

It was natural then for me to feel a strong attachment to my little brother, Paul. He was little and could be manipulated into taking my side. With a few kind words from his big sister, he could be talked into being a faithful sidekick. He was born before my third birthday and although I have no real memory of being asked to look after him, we were probably paired up to keep each other busy and out of the way while Mom baked, cooked, washed and ironed for the family.

I believe that Paul and I were so close that, not only did we share toys and playtime, but we also were somewhat jealous of each other, when it came to having to share attention from our parents. I know that we bickered and, one time in particular Paul accused Mom of always sticking up for me, at which time he stormed out of the back door and headed across the field. I remember thinking that maybe I had been unfair, since Paul had gotten so upset. Mom didn't seem so concerned, on the other hand, and, after what seemed to be an awfully long time, Paul came back acting as though he had never been gone. I guess mothers know their children best!

Paul was entered into the first grade following his fifth birthday in February. So, we grew up feeling as though we were much closer in age than we actually were. Being he was younger than most of the other boys in his grade in school, he didn't catch up in size with the majority of them, until he was a senior in high school. His size didn't keep him from playing football and other activities like his older brothers. What he lacked in size he made up for in grit and determination. Unlike his brothers, he was drafted into the high school choir. In other words, if there was any reason to believe that there was a student possessing a good voice by virtue of a family history in music, he was ferreted out and persuaded to try out for the choir, or in some cases, the band. Our music director, Mr. Solie, rightly assumed that the boys in our family had an ear for music, too, after I had joined the choir. The director knew our family and thought I could sing like my cousin, Twyla. So, I became a soloist in the school choir and Paul followed his big sister into choir as a tenor.

Getting back to Paul, we didn't hang around together with the same friends, but we crossed paths on a regular basis as we moved about town. He had a habit of staying out after curfew. Since he was still too young to have a driver's license, his friends would let him out of their car at the end of the driveway. He would walk up to the house, shinny up the tree next to the house, step onto the roof of the porch, and crawl in through the window. From there he would creep down the hall and into his bedroom. No one would probably have ever discovered his escapades, but for the fact that one night, he stepped onto my sister's bed and startled her.

When Dad died, Paul was still in high school, and had just turned seventeen. We were all so unprepared for this abrupt end to our normal lives. Dave had finished his 2 year stint in the Marines, was going to college and working part-time. Roger had completed his 4 years in the Navy and was married with 2 little girls, living and working in Minneapolis. Roger and his family moved out to the farm to take over the operation along with Paul. But, this was only temporary. So, at the end of the year's farm season, Mom rented out the farm and moved into a house in town. She would later sell the farm and the equipment. Paul registered at one of the state colleges where he finished out the first semester. Paul was not a dedicated student and, at the end of that semester, he headed to Minneapolis to get a job. He went to work at Sears in their shipping and receiving department, and before long, married his high school sweetheart and moved into an apartment.

Paul worked in several different jobs over the next few years. After their first child, Paula, was born, he was ready to spread his wings a little farther and applied for and was awarded a position with a mortgage company. I think his first assignment was repossessing homes that had been foreclosed on. But, this began his life in the real estate world. He advanced quickly and sometime around the age of 30, he had accomplished what takes many their whole lives to achieve. By this time, also, he had two more daughters, Jennifer and Kelli, and lived in a home in the suburbs.

Paul was an entrepreneur in the true sense of the word. Nothing seemed to be too big for him to handle. Sadly, his marriage fell apart and his life changed somewhat. He moved into a condominium, nice, although not luxurious. Later, he and his significant other, Sue, bought a house on a small lake south of Minneapolis. He had a boat that he enjoyed riding on the lake, with his children and grandchildren. He and Sue loved to entertain and had wonderful outdoor barbeques at times that I was there visiting. There would be boat rides, lawn games and family get-togethers.

Paul's grandson, Mitch, nearly died as an infant from shaken baby syndrome. Apparently, when Mitch was left in his father's care, he was shaken so hard by his father that he was brain damaged. Paul and Mitch's grandmother, Aryls, traveled with Mitch and his mother, Kelli, to Washington state and Florida, hoping to get help for the little boy. Paul spent an untold amount of money and time in an attempt to help Mitch. However, today Mitch is a teenager in a wheelchair, not able to speak or to feed himself. He is a beautiful boy, and, just by being in this world, has touched so many people and has brought out the goodness and love in others. Mitch's father was brought to trial and sentenced to the maximum time in the state prison for his misdeed, but his punishment was nothing compared to the life sentence that he put on Mitch.

After the death of Roger, our oldest brother, who died much too young at the age of 47, Paul and Dave grew closer and closer. They shared a lot of the same things, as had Roger and Dave. They shared the love of hunting, fishing, and horseback riding. They were brothers in the best sense of the word, showing deep respect, love and concern for each other. Brothers share a special closeness that you can actually feel in the air when you're around them.

Paul suffered with a lot of health issues. He inherited the family genes that present circulatory problems. After a stroke a number of years ago that landed him at the Mayo Clinic in a coma, his kidneys suffered. He came out of the coma, but it soon became apparent that a kidney transplant was necessary for him to get away from dialysis. I took the tests to be a possible donor, but his doctors wanted to find a younger donor, if possible. His son-in-law, Scott, stepped up and was found to be a viable donor. Surgery to transplant one of Scott's kidneys to Paul was successful and allowed Paul to live an additional four years.

While Paul fought to survive, his body rebelled. While his heart remained strong, his lungs would not allow him to breathe with ease. A walk from one room to the next had become difficult for him. My granddaughter, Sarah, and I were driving on our way to Minnesota when Dave called to tell us Paul had died that morning. My plan to visit with Paul, for what I expected to be the last time, changed in that moment. Sarah and I arrived in time to attend his funeral early in June of last year. I miss him, of course, but realize that he was tired of living in the way that he had for the last few weeks and months of his life. I am so thankful that, when I think of Paul, I remember us as little kids out in the playhouse, among the trees, in the backyard. Nothing will ever erase those memories!

FARM NEIGHBORS
Living in a Neighborhood of Friends

⌇

There is something so comforting about having neighbors. Neighbors are people who are not necessarily family or even friends. Neighbors are the people who notice a strange car in your driveway or who find your pet when it has strayed from your yard. I might go on a trip and need someone such as a neighbor to feed my dog or check on my house, or perhaps water some flowers. I pick up the mail for my neighbors when they are gone for a few days and, in appreciation they bring me a pan of blueberry muffins. Small but significant kindnesses. We have become so accustomed to hiring a service to manage things for us that we forget the pleasure we get by being neighbors. We used to welcome neighbors with open and trusting arms when they moved in nearby. Now, it seems that our first reaction is to be watchful, wondering what kind of people they might be. I'm guilty of forming an opinion of strangers based on my first impression of them and I must admit that I am sometimes too hasty. Some might think that our feelings toward our neighbors are a reflection of the area in which we live. I think that it has more to do with the times. We have come to distrust before trusting, due in part, I think, to the attention of the media given to the physical and verbal attacks of people on one another. In addition, most of us are so busy working, commuting and planning for our next vacation that we have forgotten to come outside of our air-conditioned homes to chat with our next door neighbors. My memories of neighbors as a child include the ones that the women of the household shared in so many ways. We had an abundance of apples that my mother offered to the neighbor wives. A neighbor had a beautiful strawberry patch and shared some with my mother. There were countless recipes that were exchanged and ideas or household hints for shortcuts or time-saving ways of doing the ordinary tasks. These are typical of good neighbors of today. I have, in the past, when they were still planting a garden, received garden vegetables from one of my neighbors. Likewise, my husband loved to garden and, at that time offered produce to friends and neighbors, and I have shared figs and pears, from time to time, when it has been a productive year.

What I remember from my childhood, about the farm and neighbors, was what was known as "exchange work." One of the main events of the summer harvesting was the harvesting of the grain. After the farmer had cut the grain and bound the bundles of grain with a binder, he would form shocks (a stack) using 6 to 8 bundles to a group. The shocks were arranged in a teepee shaped formation by stacking the bundles with the grain end up and leaning against each other. When all of the grain had been put into shocks, and we made sure that all were completely dry, the threshing process would begin. One of the neighbors, or maybe a partnership of a couple of the neighbors, owned a threshing machine. As the fields would ripen, the neighbors would come together at the first field and pitch the cut grain shocks onto hay racks. The hay rack was pulled by a team of horses who brought the wagon load to the threshing machine parked in the farmer's barnyard. There the stalks were separated from the grain. The grain, having been caught in a wagon, would be taken to the grain elevator in town and sold to the cooperative. Some of the grain was stored in the granary for feed for the animals. The straw was left in a straw stack to be used for bedding for the farm animals in the wintertime. Again, I remember the smells of this whole operation from beginning to end and am reminded of how soft the straw feels on the feet when you jump in it. My older brothers were not yet teen-agers when they formed one of the teams in bringing the hay racks to the threshing machine operated by Dad. It was a man's job handled by boys 11 and 13 years of age.

Later, the threshing machine was replaced by the combine. A farmer could do the whole operation by himself with the new procedure. The field of grain was cut and separated by the machine pulled behind a tractor. Later, a baling machine was brought onto the field to pick up and bale the straw that lay on the ground. Likewise, the baler was used to bale hay, making that part of the feeding operation more time and space efficient. Life on the farm in those early days required a lot of muscle and dedication, putting in long days, pitting the farmers' strength and endurance against the whims of nature. Here we witness the change in the social structure of the farm. With the coming of bigger and better equipment, the need for assistance in many areas of farming was lessened or eliminated.

Not to be overlooked are the occasions when a farmer was ill or may have been injured and unable to get his work completed. Neighbors would organize and come to the home of the disabled farmer to do his work for him. Sometimes a farmer would leave his own unfinished harvesting to join a group of good neighbors. The women in the neighborhood would bring food and run errands to keep the momentum going. Let's face it, there wasn't any Workman's Compensation to fall back on. Without family and the people who lived nearby to provide support in an emergency, the farm might have been in jeopardy.

There was no trade school to teach a farmer all that he needed to know in order to operate a farm. Not only did my Dad oversee the crops in the field and the animals in the barns, but he was his own mechanic and blacksmith most of the time. If a part broke or needed replacing, Dad would either make the repair himself or take a broken metal piece to the blacksmith to be welded or have a new piece made. He sharpened his own mower blades and did small carpentry repairs and fixed electrical problems. If a tire went flat on a tractor, he would take it off and take it to the garage to be fixed and just hope that he wouldn't have to bear the expense of having to replace one of those big, costly tires.

By Dad's example we learned how to take a tire off the bicycle and put a patch on the inner tube. We knew how to put a chain back on and tighten a loose screw before a tire or a fender fell off. I don't think that any of us wanted to admit that we weren't knowledgeable enough to fix things ourselves.

Dad always said that farming was a gamble. A farmer invested time and money in planting, tilling and harvesting the annual crop. If there wasn't enough rain, or if there was a hail storm, or if there was too much rain, or if the autumn frost came too early, it would be a poor year for the farmer. There wasn't enough crop insurance to cover all the possibilities of disaster. If you wanted to be a farmer you had to be ambitious, ready to put in long days and prepared to face unexpected setbacks. Most importantly, of all, a farmer has to love his job!

TOYS, GAMES AND RECREATION
Dolls, Tire Swings and Ponies

By other people's standards we probably never had many toys. One of the reasons that I am able to recall so many of our toys is, perhaps, because there were not that many to remember. Before I started school, I had the baby doll that Grandma helped to outfit with pillows for the buggy and doll crib blankets. When I was four years old, my mother had learned about a gift that I was to receive for Christmas. She told me that I was going to be so surprised with the gift that my cousin, Twyla, was making for me for Christmas. Mom said that I was really going to love my gift. I don't know what ideas I had conjured up in my head. But, when Christmas finally came, I couldn't help but let the disappointment show on my face. She had made a set of big and little sister cloth dolls for me. They were tiny little things, the largest of the two probably only six or eight inches tall. She had invested an enormous amount of time and patience into making the little dolls: embroidering the eyes, nose and mouth on the faces, and making hair from yellow yarn on their heads. She had made clothes with tiny buttons for them and added shoes made out of black satin to their feet . I know that she had put more effort into my Christmas gift than any that I have received before and since. I can't remember what she gave to Roger and Dave that year. She had made Paul a broomstick horse that he played with for a long time. I think that I had said that I wished for a doll as tall as myself that Christmas, which would probably have been around three feet tall, and had a difficult time getting over my disappointment. Maybe I was the spoiled child, after all, and not my sister, Lois, as we are still fond of telling her.

I distinctly recall a brown baby doll that was given to Dave as a toddler. He has been denying that fact for years and claims that he never had a doll. I don't remember who gave him the doll or the circumstances that brought that about, but it was, I guess, the most unusual present that any of us ever received. I figure that the doll was probably on sale since there would not have been much demand for a colored doll in that all white Scandinavian community where we lived. Paul was given a Humpty Dumpty doll as a baby gift, so we used that fact to tease him when he got a little bigger. Strange how boys don't want to acknowledge ever liking soft and cuddly things unless it's a real live puppy or a kitten.

My brothers knew how to play without a lot of toys. The times that each of them would borrow a dish towel from the kitchen to use for a cape gave them the ability to mimic their comic book heroes. They were Batman and Robin or Captain Marvel and Superman. They even let me tie a towel around my neck and run after them as Mary Marvel or Wonder Woman! As we got older, we became more adept at making our own playthings. I learned by watching my brothers how to make a bow and arrows from a willow branch and twine for the bow and split wooden shingles for the arrows. They had a cap pistol or two, but knew how to make a "rubber gun," a wooden gun that shot strips of inner tube. We played cops and robbers, cowboys and Indians and good guys and bad guys. These were the games played at home when we were little. Of course, there was always a swing hanging from a tree in the back yard. In addition to the usual rope swing with the wooden seat, we had a tire swing where you could sit and swing and spin and even let a passenger sit at the top of the tire and share the fun. At school we played tag, softball, had races and other playground games. I don't remember any of the children having a weight problem. We were constantly moving about when we were left to our own interests. Even the little one room schoolhouse playgrounds had swing sets, merry-go-rounds and gliders, where we played hard every day, weather permitting.

Entertainment didn't always require toys. We lived within walking distance of the river, allowing us to walk or ride bikes to go fishing.

The only fish we ever saw and caught were bullheads, an ugly black fish that we caught with a rod and reel or sometimes with just a willow branch, fish line and a hook. We would bring our catch back to the house and ask Mom to fry them for us for supper. The boys would clean them, cutting off the tails and those ugly heads with the whiskers. Of course, we thought that they were delicious!

Mom was so patient with all of us when we brought in some wild game for the table. The one time that she wasn't gracious about the dinner contribution was the time that Dave had shot a squirrel (or maybe it was a rabbit), and, after gutting and skinning it, bringing it to the kitchen and laying it on the table, asked Mom to fry it for him. Mom took one look and nearly became physically sick. She said that she couldn't handle it. It looked too much like a skinned monkey.

My brothers many times received Christmas gifts that were addressed to both Roger and David. They shared an electric train and an erector set as well as a basketball and tinker toys. A corner of the living room or dining room floor was usually occupied by some type of joint building project. If they ever argued or fought over any of their toys, I was not aware of their doing so. There was most likely an understanding of how these possessions would be shared and undoubtedly they were well aware of what the consequences would be if they were unable to cooperate with each other. There were the board games that were brought out in the cold season(s). We played regular checkers, Chinese Checkers, Monopoly, Caroms, Parcheesi and several others. We played the card game, Rook, and for the younger set, Old Maid and Go Fish.

It's sad, in a way, that children of today have given up so many of these past times. Today children play opposite a computer often by themselves in a roomful of others playing on another gadget. Kids sit at the same table and communicate by cell phone instead of talking directly to each other. Is it any wonder that there is a lack of communication in the world?

This is not to say that I don't appreciate my cell phone or my computer or my e-book. But, it's somehow refreshing when a member of the younger generation agrees to help put a jigsaw puzzle together, or perhaps play a game of Chinese Checkers?

THE FULLER BRUSH MAN
Never a Dull Moment

If my siblings and I were ever bored when we were little, we wouldn't have known the meaning of the word. Any time one of us slipped and muttered that there was nothing to do, we would be given something to do that we probably did not have in mind. In those days we didn't have a lot of toys to pick up, so that wasn't what we were told to do. We may have been asked to keep the baby entertained until Mom had a minute to tend to him or her. Sometimes we would be told to bring in some wood from the woodpile outside to fill the wood box. There were assignments given to us when we were big enough to help with various things. My brothers were taught from a very early age to be ready to help with the animal chores in the barn and chicken house. This was every day, no exceptions. When they were little, Roger and David had to take turns helping with the dish drying after supper while the lucky one would help Dad with the evening chores in the barn. No respectable young boy wanted to be caught drying dishes in the kitchen with his mother! There was frequently some difference of opinion regarding whose turn it was to help in the kitchen. Consequently, Mom, in her teacher mode, developed a chart that hung on the kitchen cabinet, clearly defining whose turn it was on any given day.

I remember summer days when a group of boys in the neighborhood made the trek to the bank of the slow moving river a mile or so away. They would ride bikes over the dusty gravel road. There they managed to hook some of the nasty carp that survived in the low waters, after a period of rain, making them fair game to little fishermen. I begged to go along with them, but I didn't have a bicycle of my own. They allowed me to accompany them, riding on the handle bar or crossbar of one of my brother's bikes. It was fine until they hit a small rock in the road. Then I would bounce on the metal bar and realize how uncomfortable a ride can be without a cushioned seat.

Coming back to the house from play in the afternoon, Mom would give us a snack of cookies or homemade doughnuts and Kool-Aid or lemonade. The Watkins salesman visited the homes in the countryside and my mother would buy vanilla flavoring from him and one of our favorites, orange nectar, that she would make into a refreshing summer drink. The Watkins man and the Fuller Brush man were the forerunners of the Internet of today. You didn't have to go out to shop. The rep would bring his wares to your door. A few years later, a new salesman arrived in a yellow refrigerated truck selling ice cream door to door, or should I say, farmhouse to farmhouse? We still see the yellow truck in all parts of the country with Schwan's proudly displayed on the side of the truck. This was at the time that most of the farms had a freezer in the basement. There was always room for a couple of pails of ice cream.

We worked hard and we played hard and we were rewarded with treats at the end of many of those days. One of Dad's favorites was rootbeer floats. He would surprise us in the evening by bringing home root beer and vanilla ice cream for us to enjoy. Another time we would have a big watermelon carved up into generous slices and devoured by happy and excited kids and our parents. I remember the watermelon pickles Mom would make from the peeled rinds the next day. This was my favorite pickle!

No, we weren't bored. At least, we were not bored long. There was always a branch in an apple tree where one could daydream on a hot afternoon, or as in the case of Dave, a seat high at the top of the windmill to gaze into South Dakota. At the end of the day, everyone, young and old, was asleep when our heads hit the pillow.

$\sim$

COMMUNICATIONS
Before Cell Phones and Computers

$\sim$

At a time when it is almost impossible to live through a day with-out a cell phone in one's pocket, imagine going back two or three generations when, for many of us, just having a phone on the wall of the dining room was a luxury. We left the convenience of a telephone when we moved from the farm of my birth to the little house that had very few comforts. A telephone was something that my mother had to wait for when we moved to that house, but I believe my mother had a strong voice, when it was decided which conveniences were necessary. We may not have had an indoor bathroom, but we would not be cut off from our neighbors and family.

Telephones were finally coming out that could be set on a desk or hall table, but ours was the wooden box type that was attached to the wall. There were no dials or numbers appearing anywhere on the surface. We were part of a "party line." This meant that two or three other households shared the same time on the phone. Before making a call, one had to pick up the receiver first to listen, to make sure that no one was already on the line. If a dial tone was heard, we could call anyone on our line by ringing the correct number of long or short rings assigned to that party. We, of course, had our own "ring" to an-swer to. If it had our signal, we would answer. If the rings belonged to another party, we would ignore the call, knowing that the call was not for us. There were sometimes nosey folks sharing our party line who would listen to other peoples' conversations. The illegal listeners were called rubber-necks, people with long inquisitive necks. To call someone other than the people on our party line, we would ring one long ring, probably two or three rotations of the crank. Doing this would signal the operator, who would respond with "number, please." One of my mother's favorite nieces was a telephone operator before being married. She worked in one of the neighboring towns and seems to have considered herself pretty self-sufficient and wasted no time in buying a new, low riding Buick. It was one of those with a whole lot of chrome on it, a real show car. I am not sure, but think that it was blue or black, with the chrome-encircled openings in the front fenders. I remember Dad commenting on her purchase, saying something to the effect that she had bought something that she couldn't afford. Dad didn't believe in buying anything you couldn't afford, and he knew that she had to take out a loan in order to finance this big car.

Our means of communicating with family and friends at a distance was by letter. A long-distance telephone call was practically unknown. Mom kept up a correspondence with my Dad's sisters who lived at a distance, particularly those in South Dakota, by letter. Often times one of these aunts would write to another, then after adding her news on the bottom or on another piece of stationery, would forward the letter on to the next, until someone decided that all the family news had been shared with everyone. This would keep everyone in touch until the next family reunion, wedding, or funeral, which would bring everyone together.

When I was in elementary school there was a program started to encourage pen pals. I don't remember how this was organized, but I was a pen pal for some time with a girl my age, named Phyllis, who lived in Huron, South Dakota. I don't remember either of us having much to say about our lives to each other, but I recall how exciting it was to get a letter delivered to me from her even though the only way I knew her was from a poorly taken snapshot that she had sent to me with her first letter. I like to think that kids would really enjoy having that kind of correspondence today. It would certainly make them unique from the other kids who friend each other on Face Book.

My father was an active member of the community, in church and the schools where we, his children, attended. He was a trustee in church and was the chairman of the school board when I was in elementary school and he kept a close watch on what went on in the school. The Minneapolis Tribune was delivered to our mailbox every day and was read in its entirety by my father from front to back. We had to be quiet while the news was delivered on the radio two or three times a day. We were current in the news of the neighborhood and of the world.

We didn't have the technology to text each other, like the young people of today. The closest we came to that practice was passing notes back and forth to each other in school, hoping not to get caught!

Norwegian Influences
Being Raised in a Discriminating Environment

G rowing up in a family whose entire tree contained only Norwegians and in a community of a majority of Norwegians, it would have been impossible for my generation not to develop some of the skills and habits of our ancestors. Next to pride in our country, we were proud of our stalwart Viking background. Perhaps Viking is an exaggeration of who we are. The Vikings were more likely to be aggressive, whereas we felt ourselves to be kind, strong, and devoted to our church, community and country.

I don't remember a time when Mom and Dad failed to go to the polls to vote in all of the elections: local, state and national. They took the issues seriously, going to hear any politician who appeared locally and scanning the newspapers and listening closely to promises and oaths that were being made. At that time, even in the early elementary grades, we were encouraged to delve into topics of the time, nationally and internationally. We were privileged to receive The Weekly Reader and later Current Events after which we discussed the news that we had read. We may not have had the internet, but we spent time digesting the events of the day, just a few days later than the actual event. We had regional contests, followed by county contests, where we were judged on our knowledge in current events as well as our spelling skills.

Our grandparents brought with them to America dishes that our parents loved and gave to us. The all time favorite in our family was (and still is) potato dumplings, known as klub in Norwegian. Anyone who thinks of the potato as a food staple will love dumplings. To prepare them, raw potatoes are ground and mixed in a bowl with flour and seasoned with salt and pepper. Having achieved the proper consistency, one forms a small baseball sized portion into a ball, drops into boiling water and cooks until the dumplings are done. Another method that Mom used, was to loosely stuff the raw mix into a cotton bag about five or six inches long, tie the end closed, and drop the bag into the boiling water. When done, the bag is cut open and large slices of dumplings are served on the dinner plate. This delicacy along with a pork chop or another cut of pork and a large pat of butter will please any good Norwegian or Norwegian-want-to-be.

Christmas brings out the best in cooks, regardless of ancestry. We could hardly wait to taste the treats Mom created just for the holidays. Top among the list of goodies for us was the lefsa. Lefsa is a light bread made with cream and fried on the top of the stove. At least that is how it was done when I was very small. With the coming of the electric stove, the transfer was made to an electric lefsa grill. This round grill was made especially for frying lefsa and produced the same results. There are two kinds of lefsa, one using mashed potatoes in the mix, and the other plain using only flour, which I preferred. Those who liked the potato kind better, would eat them with butter and sugar, making them much sweeter. I liked the other better, spreading them only with butter. Not much farther down the list of preferred breads is flat bread. Stores carry flat bread under a variety of brands on specialty shelves, but nothing compares to the homemade flat bread. There again, two types were made, one with white flour and another using whole wheat flour. Once again, I had my preference, liking the whole wheat flour variety better, but I loved both!

Maybe Norwegians are not the only nationality to enjoy the fruits of slaughter to the extent that our family did. We all liked the bruklub or blood dumplings. Here again, potatoes were incorporated into a family favorite. In addition to the potatoes and flour, fresh blood from a butchered pig was included in the recipe. Some of us didn't like it after learning of the secret ingredient, even though we recognized that blood is a part of eating meat. After the dumplings had been cooked in their cloth casing and chilled, slices of the round loaf would be fried and eaten with butter. It really astounds me that my ancestors lived such long lives with a diet that contained so much butter and other fattening ingredients.

It seems as though my Mom's and Dad's families both used a large amount of molasses in baking and cooking. Mom's homemade baked beans were so good and that was because of the addition of the molasses and brown sugar. The cookies my grandmothers made were rolled out flat on a floured board, cut into circles and baked. I remember my Dad's mother using a coffee cup held upside down to cut out the circles. She didn't need things like special measuring cups or spoons as utensils from the cupboard worked just as well. Of course, it's not the amount we use, but the proportions of the ingredients. The tops would be sprinkled with sugar and were especially delicious when eaten warm from the oven. Dad's parents lived next door to a soda bottling plant when they retired from the farm. They kept a supply of "Grapette" and "Orange Crush" pop for the grandchildren when we visited, which complemented the molasses or white cookies as our snacks.

Minnesotans are noted for their Scandinavian brogue and expressions. Who hasn't heard "you betcha" in relation to the people of Minnesota? "Uff-da" can be translated into the Southern dialect as "my land" or "bless your heart." So much can be said with so few words provided we can interpret the meaning of what we intended to say. When I was growing up we pretended to imitate the older generation by saying "Are yoou in town today, tooo?" being sure to drag the words out in an exaggerated fashion. We had to be reminded to say "yes" rather than "yah." Mom, as a former teacher, was a constant monitor of our speech. She was quick to correct us if the wrong verb slipped out. I have had to consciously remind myself not to be too critical of another's missteps in English. I realize that some improper English is for effect, so I try not to pay too much attention to those bloopers. I don't cringe as much as I once did hearing overly gross errors in speech habits. After all, it's much more important to capture the thought of the speaker than the choice of words. If we want to know how people are feeling we must allow them to tell us in their words, not ours. I admit to fracturing our official language from time to time, when sometimes my rambling tongue takes over my mind and my better judgment.

One of my prized possessions is a Bible written in Norwegian that was given to my mother at the time of her confirmation by her pastor. I admit that I can't read a word of it other than the names of the books in the Bible and some of those I question. It serves as a reminder of my family's roots and tells me that I need to treasure these connections to the past and it also shall serve as a bridge to future generations. How else can we know who we are, if we don't know where we came from?

My grandparents and parents gave my siblings and me a strong sense of who we were. Along with strict morals and dedication to our place in this democracy, we were afforded a knowledge and pride in our ancestry. We joked about people of dissimilar backgrounds, such as the Swedes and the Germans. Our integration came when the descendants of immigrants married outside of their parents' pure genes as Norwegians married Swedes and Lutherans married Catholics. It should be no surprise that it has taken generations for the people in this country to begin to learn to live in harmony with one another. The more we change, the more we stay the same?

PHOTOS

MY PARENTS BEFORE ME: (top) Wanda's mother Olga Dahl Bjornlie and father Olaf Bjornlie have their first portraits made in the same studio just a couple of months apart; (middle, l-r) Olga's confirmation c. 1917; Olga's high school graduation c. 1920; Olaf and Olga marriage c. 1933; (bottom) Olga c. 1904.

MY PARENTS BEFORE
ME: (top, clockwise) Olga
Dahl Bjornlie and father
Hans Dahl; Rebecca and
Hans Dahl; Olaf with David
and Wanda; Roger, Paul and
Wanda with hired girl Alice
c. 1942; and Olga with baby
Wanda c. 1939.

THE EARLY YEARS: (from top left, clockwise) Wanda as a toddler; siblings David, Wanda and Roger bundled up for the Minnesota cold; Wanda (in the tub), David, Roger and Paul; the Bjornlie siblings in Dawson (Roger, David, Wanda, Paul and Lois); and first best friends Paul and Wanda c. 1946.

THE EARLY YEARS: (from top left, clockwise) Bjornlie siblings ready for a cousin's wedding; picnic with Dad, Mom, David, Roger and baby Wanda; Wanda with cousins Charles and Carolyn; Lois and Paul at Lake Itasca; paper dolls in the forties; and family picnic with Dad, Mom, Roger, Wanda, David and baby Paul.

THE EARLY YEARS: Wanda's profound interest in writing is demonstrated at the early age of eight years old, winning grand prize at the 1947 Minnesota State Fair for a story about a family trip to South Dakota.

A Valentine Party

Upon Valentine day we had a party at the schoolhouse in the evening. At the party we had movies. One movie which I saw on this evening was about paper hangers. The paper hanger tried to straighten the paper, but the paper would always roll back. Then a man with a beard came and got beard in the paste. So the paper hanger cut off his beard so as to loosen it from the paper. The man was going run his hand over the beard when he found it wasn't there. A little later he was in the way so a

THE EARLY YEARS: Wanda continues her award-winning writing by winning first prize at the Lac Qui Parle County Fair in 1949 for an essay about a Valentine's Day party.

ANIMALS WHOM I HAVE KNOWN: (from top) Family friend Wanda Larson with Captain; Paul, Lois (on Captain) and Wanda; Paul, David and Wanda with farm puppies; Lois with the kitty she took to school for a portrait.

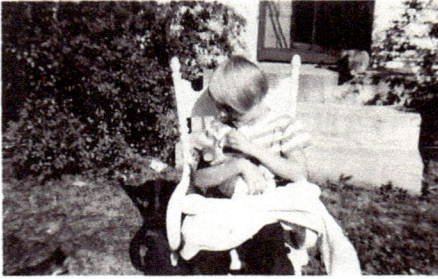

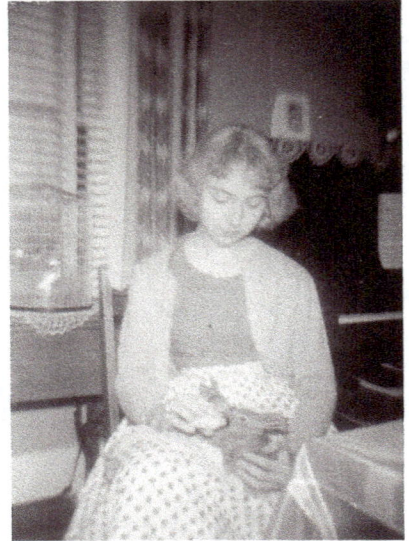

ANIMALS WHOM I HAVE
KNOWN and THE TEENAGE
YEARS: (from top left, clockwise)
Wanda with Paul and Lois; Wanda
bottle feeding a baby rabbit; Wanda
with the cats; Wanda as a 'tween; Paul
and Lois with the family dog; and
Lois nursing a cat.

MOVING ON: Wanda singing at the wedding of her cousin Aletrice and Harlan in 1959 with friend Joann Roisen accompanying on the organ.

FARM LIFE IN THE FIFTIES: (top) Dad and our neighbor, Helmer Helgeson, Dave on the tractor, Lois with her back to the camera in the jeans and plaid shirt and Helmer's son, Ronnie sitting on the ground; (bottom) An old Farmall tractor used for a variety of tasks on the farm.

TRAVELING BACK: (top) Aerial view of the Bjornlie farm in Dawson, Minnesota, circa 1955; (bottom) the Bjornlie farm present day.

TRAVELING BACK: (top) House in which Olaf Bjornlie was born in 1903; (bottom left) the barn used for storing hay in the hay mow and housing farm animals in the cold winter months; (bottom right) the granary and chicken house.

TRAVELING BACK: (top) Farm on which Wanda and her family lived from 1945-48; (middle) the grove of trees that was once filled with apple trees; (bottom) an old wagon by the silo; (opposite page) Main Street Dawson today.

GROWING UP LUTHERAN
It Was in Our DNA

❧

Faith is the first word that I think of when I pause to remember my early religious training. Trust is the second word. I had faith in what I was being taught and trust in the ones teaching me. Although we had friends who attended churches of other denominations, our entire extended family were Lutherans. Staying faithful to the Lutheran Church was as important as being faithful to one's spouse. We never gave a thought about leaving the church of our upbringing. Even though a couple of friends and I visited two or three other churches, as teenagers, we were just curious about them, and had no plans or inclinations toward visiting more than once. We, of course, believed we were in the best possible place.

As a toddler I accompanied my mother to her monthly meetings of the Ladies Aid Society and other smaller groups or circles. I can picture myself in the basement of the little country church sitting beside Mom and waiting for the business meeting and devotions to be over so we could have the refreshments of sandwiches and sweets, coffee and Kool-Aid. I can vaguely recall discussions of clothes drives for the victims of the war. They talked about the poor little children in the war-torn countries and of the refugees that we would help. There would be fundraisers to support the missionary efforts to Africa, China and Eastern Europe. Meals would be served to ticket buyers, cookbooks assembled and sold so that Bibles could be distributed overseas. When we didn't clean our plates at mealtime, we were reminded of the starving children in China. Remember, this was the time of World War II and everyone's civil and godly efforts were heightened.

Later, as a teenager, I attended meetings with my peers at Luther League. I'm not sure what our good works were, but it did give us a place to go and a way to keep us out of trouble. There was one summer evening at Luther League where we were divided into teams and given a list for a scavenger hunt. We had a time limit, but it must have been a long time limit since we ran all over town, knocking on doors, asking people for a piece of blue string or a red pencil or some such thing. Later we would report back to church and after the winner was proclaimed, we would do what teenagers do best: we ate hamburgers and cookies and downed bottles of Coca Cola or some kind of pop.

"Has everybody done their Sunday School lesson?" was the first question we were asked after finishing our supper on Saturday night. We were in Sunday School every Sunday morning at 9:45, for assembly where we would sing songs, pray for the unfortunate and for each other. Then we were off to our classes with our Sunday School books to recite our Bible verses and review our Bible stories. The services in the sanctuary started at 11:00 A.M. with the choir in their black robes coming down the aisle to the choir loft with everyone singing Holy, Holy, Holy. It was such a proud moment the first time we were allowed to join the adult choir when we entered high school.

Beginning the seventh grade also meant the start of two years of confirmation classes for those of us who were Lutherans. We would meet with our pastor every Saturday morning from September through May to become more active and responsible members of our church. We learned the creeds and studied the history of Lutheranism. We had open discussions on our beliefs and interpretations of the Bible. At the end of our classes we would be honored on a Sunday in May where each of us was given questions by the pastor to answer in front of the congregation. Only after satisfying these steps were we allowed to take part in communion and to take our place among the adults in the church. If only becoming an adult was that easy!

If you were a member of a Lutheran church you were expected to attend Vacation Bible School for a week in the summer. Everyone was ready for summer vacation from school, but we didn't have complete freedom until Bible School was over. We were there in the mornings, after which we could go to the swimming pool or, in the case of our family, go home to have lunch and offer our help on the farm. Usually, someone (Mom) would have to deliver us to the church and pick us up at noon. I'm thinking that Mom was ready at the end of the week to start the real summer vacation as much as we were. In Bible School we did a lot of memorizing of Bible verses during the week. Every day we were adding new verses and reviewing the ones from earlier in the week. Old Testament stories were a big part of the lessons that we learned. We became familiar with the prophets and their roles in the history of the Jewish people, the foundation of our Christian faith.

I remember a few times when I rode my bike to Bible School. This was when I was old enough to be trusted on the streets of town on a bike. I would take the road out of town that paralleled the railroad tracks since that would have been the road less traveled. I was discouraged from riding my bike after the day I was on my way home and was spotted by the neighbor just to the north of our house. He was on his tractor, probably cultivating, since it would have been the time for that farming operation. When he saw me he gestured a peddling motion with his hands and I was repulsed by his attention. Several years later, when I heard that he had left his wife and children for another woman, I felt that my feelings about him were instinctively correct. This was the only person that I can say that I distrusted and it was purely just a sick gut feeling. I have learned to be cautious when encountering people for the first time. If I get a feeling of something wrong, I think it is better to go with my gut feeling and remain a stranger until I can feel comfortable. Admittedly, my first impressions, good or bad, may be wrong. I have changed my opinions from time to time.

My parents grew up in families who were active in church. My paternal grandfather was a lay minister in the little country church. He would serve in the pulpit when the pastor was not there. When I was small, I remember Grandpa preaching in Norwegian. It seems that the older members who could speak or understand Norwegian loved to hear the sermon in that language. He could have preached in English, but answered the request for a Norwegian Sunday. Dad was on the board of trustees for a time when I was a teenager. Part of his duties included counting the collection at the end of the service. We tried to be patient, waiting for Dad to come out of church and drive us home to the traditional Sunday dinner of beef or pork that had been roasting in the oven while we were in church. Mom was putting her new electric range with the oven timing devise to practical use. It only took a few minutes to have our noontime dinner on the table after we got home. I can almost smell the rich, brown gravy today as I recall satisfying my hunger after spending the Sunday morning in church. My favorite Sunday repast to this day is one of beef pot roast with potatoes, carrots and onions, a side of coleslaw and pie for dessert. Of course, nobody could cook like Mom!

Our family sat in the same spot in the same pew, every Sunday. We were surrounded by other families or couples who had their favorite place picked out. We were always on the second pew from the back of the church in the middle section on the left facing the church. We could tell at a glance who was missing from church by the unoccupied seats. Mom and Dad separated us from each other to make sure that we behaved. As we got older we were allowed to sit with friends, providing that we didn't embarrass our parents. We were careful to sit down near the front, as far away as we could get from them. I must say that we rarely, if ever, had to be reprimanded for being bad. By bad, I mean whispering during the sermon or showing too much interaction with our friends when we should have been listening. We knew that misbehaving in church would not be taken lightly. As prospective confirmands, we were obligated to take notes during the sermon as topics for discussion in class the following Saturday morning.

I'm thankful for the religious upbringing we were given. We never questioned why we were going to church. Attending church, like going to school, was not questioned.

THINGS THAT MY MOTHER TAUGHT ME

Wonder Woman Extraordinaire

M om could have written the book on multi-tasking, a term not yet coined, but certainly practiced every day as she maintained her role as farm wife and mother. She could do the laundry while she planned and prepared three meals a day for a family of seven, in addition to two snacks between meals which we justifiably called lunches. (These lunches were made up of sandwiches and a couple of cookies or a piece of cake.) At the same time she was performing all of the duties of seamstress, nurse, counselor and arbitrator. She was our judge and our confessor, soft and strict, and our go-between when we needed permission from Dad for a special request (i.e., "It's okay with me if Dad says it's okay.").

I have not been able to figure out how my mother found the time to do all of the many different things that she did. Raising the five of us to become pretty decent individuals must surely have been a daunting task. She had very few conveniences to rely on. After all, most of the modern appliances hadn't hit the stores when she raised us.

Wash day was always on Monday. Mom, for a period of three years, had to go out to the little wash house to do the laundry. Water had to be heated and carried from the house. I expect that Dad helped with that part of the laundry, although I was too young to remember (or perhaps I was still in the bed). After the clothes were washed, rinsed, and rung out with the Maytag washer, they were hung out on clothes lines in the back yard. In the coldest part of the winter, the clothes were brought into this little farmhouse and hung

91

up on clothes racks to dry. When the youngest was a baby, there were five of us under the age of ten. It's hard to figure out where all the clothes for this family had room to dry!

There had to be a great deal of organization to keep things going. Tuesdays were reserved for ironing and baking bread. In between times, there was mending and sewing. Mom made most of the dresses that I wore. Clothes were mended until they only suitable for rags. Buttons were replaced and socks mended. Little boys' overalls were patched on the knees. There were skinned knees, bumps on the head and nosebleeds that required immediate attention. In the evenings, Mom was there to help and supervise the homework. It's a wonder she was awake to say bedtime prayers with us.

I remember only one time that I witnessed Mom making homemade lye soap. I would have been 6 or 7 and we were sitting on the grass in the back yard. I thought it was an exciting thing to do. I'm not sure how Mom felt about it, but I recall her remarking that homemade soap was the best for getting clothes clean. I was reminded from time to time to stay back to keep from getting burned from the lye as I watched the mixture of lard and lye being stirred. It was poured into a pan, and, after cooling, was cut into bars with a sharp knife. I later watched Mom shaving soap from the bar into the washing machine. I wish that I could know how many times that she actually made soap, as I remember just this one time. I think that it would be a pretty safe guess for me to assume that her mother, my grandmother, helped her the first time when she stayed with us when I was a toddler.

Mom knew how to do a lot of things. She seemed not to be afraid to try anything. There was a time that she did some dry cleaning out in the yard. Why she felt it necessary to do that, I can't imagine, since, as far as I know, there was always a dry cleaning establishment in town. Maybe she figured that she could do it as well and would save money this way.

One of the luxuries Mom enjoyed was taking snapshots of all of us as we were growing up. The only camera I knew her to own while we were children was a Kodak Brownie box camera. Sometime along the way before my earliest recollections, the camera had been dropped and allowed a little light exposure into one corner of the camera. This was as good as Mom's signature on her photographs, if there was ever any doubt as to whose camera captured an image. A piece of white adhesive tape covered the defect in the little black box, but Mom didn't seem to mind the imperfection of this, her personal possession. Keep in mind that this was before the day of duct tape and all of the other stronger tapes of today. We never knew when we would be called on to pose for a picture. Anytime that Mom decided that we looked particularly nice she would line us up for a picture update. Film and developing was not cheap, according to Mom, therefore she was the only one qualified to "man" the camera. Without that Brownie camera there would not have been nearly as many pictures of us to look at today.

Nothing stayed the same in our house. There were always subtle changes throughout the house. Sometimes the changes were not so subtle, especially if you started to lower yourself into a chair that was no longer there. Mom might ask us what color we would like to have in our bedroom. She didn't want every room to be alike. I always chose blue for my room, so my brothers ended up with yellow or green. I might get home from school one day and find new curtains in my bedroom. The kitchen was likely to get a new coat of paint in the spring. The color would be different. It might go from yellow to green and back to yellow again, but I don't remember her ever painting a new coat of the same color. Uncle Rob sold paint at the furniture store so she would get a discount (most likely a big one), which allowed her to do a lot of painting. She would take on huge painting projects such as painting the living room and dining room. Sometimes, as we got older, she would allow us to help her, but I think that she really loved what she was doing. The seasons called for rearranging the furniture, upstairs and down. Mom's excuse for the changes was that she liked one arrangement, but had to change for the winter months, moving the sofa and dressers and such away from the heating vents. I believe she just loved change.

One of Mom's occupations during the summer months was that of gardener. She did everything but mow the lawn. That job belonged to us, her children. We had one of those push mower jobs, no motor, just push. We would take turns with each one of us taking one or two turns around the yard, so it wasn't that tough of a job. There were always at least two of us assigned to the task. In the garden, Mom planted the seeds, weeded and picked. Later she canned beans, tomatoes, peas, carrots, beets and made pickles from cucumbers. In the morning, if Mom wasn't in the kitchen when we got up, chances were that she was out weeding or picking strawberries or raspberries before the weather became too hot out in the sun. She seemed to enjoy the solitude of the garden. Rarely did she ask for our help in that arena. Then came the jam and jelly making, canning of fruits and the corn picking and canning.

Mom was a strict disciplinarian, although, as my brothers got older, they were able to turn her scowl into a smile with a fake show of alarm at her disapproving words. Her final warning came with a stern, "If you're going to fight, go outside!" Failing to close the door completely, we were admonished with, "Close the door! You weren't born in a barn." She stood just under five feet, four inches tall, but used her training as a teacher to stand up to her children who all were soon taller than she. I don't believe she ever uttered a "darn" or "doggone." She was forever dignified and a lady. The only time she wore a pair of pants was in the winter on days that she still hung the wash out on the line, and then wore the only pair of pants I knew her to own, under her dress, to come off as soon as she returned to the house.

It seems that Mom was forever busy and never complained about all that she had to do. She was proud of a neat and clean house. She never mopped a floor, she washed the floors, on her hands and knees with a rag and a pail of soapy water. She declared that this was the only way to get into the corners.

I can still hear her saying, "Don't come in. The floor is still wet." We would retreat and come in a few minutes later or go in by another door. She never owned a dishwasher. Usually Mom took charge of the washing and we took turns drying, oftentimes arguing about whose turn it was. Only when the dishes had been put away and the kitchen floor swept was Mom ready to relax at the end of the day. The next day, she would be ready to start over, once again, getting everyone up for school or work, fixing our breakfasts, packing lunches and, more than likely, breathing a sigh of relief when we left the house.

Her sister, Nora, called her every morning. They would speak for only a few minutes to find out from each other how they were that day. Perhaps Mom sat down at the piano for a few minutes of relaxation. That thought pleases me.

One-Room Schools
Random Thoughts and Favorite Things

❧

Getting an education, on any level, is simply filling your head up with as many facts and fantasies as possible. I had several different teachers of varying ages and qualifications. The youngest was not many years older than her oldest students. She was my first grade teacher at the school in District 25 and I have no idea of what happened to her after that first year of her teaching career. I have secretly hoped that perhaps she married and was able to minister to her own children. Even at the age of six, I was able to sense that she would be happier somewhere else. The teacher the next year was a little older and had several years of experience in her field. She was quick to give praise and not reluctant to hand out reproofs when needed. I don't believe that I ever had a teacher who was incapable of teaching, but some stand out in my mind as caring just a little more than others.

Considering the size of our elementary schools, we had access to most, if not all, of the opportunities of other children at the time. Most of us had a good time in school, even though we thought it would be unnatural not to complain about math, or history, or homework. I remember getting new books: clean, fresh, good smelling books. One of my favorites was Wagon Wheels, a novel disguised as a history book. I must have been in about the fourth grade when we studied that one. Another one from the same time was Faces and Places. It was fascinating to enter into the countries of South America or Africa as a child being portrayed in the geography book. It took us to countries all over the globe and told us of the languages spoken in different places, sometimes inserting a word or two in Spanish or Italian. At that time we recognized that all children the world over were more the same than we were different. We learned that children in other countries ate foods that were often seasoned differently from those we were accustomed to, but families were still families. Even though sometimes their skin color was not the same as ours and their homes may have been built in a different style, we all took pride in being a part of loving family. We had another series of books, The Quinlan Books, which included Coast to Coast. I'm not sure of other families, but all of our family loved to read and devoted much of our spare time reading for pure pleasure.

Sometimes we are affected by others to a degree that we don't realize at the time. This is how I feel about a young boy my age who attended school with us. He was the only child of a couple whose farmhouse was only a mile from our house. He was quiet and with-drawn. He never volunteered to speak up in class. He didn't appear to want to interact with others, yet he drew attention to himself when he would bite his fingernails constantly. I remember the teacher attempt-ing to reason with him, but it only made the matter worse. When he wasn't biting his nails, he was chewing on the calluses on the palms of his hands. I have to believe that his father made a habit of beating him and belittling him. I know that he was expected by his father to do a man's job when he was only nine or 10 years old. I can't say what my Mom and Dad thought about this family. I don't think that my Dad was very complimentary, at least by Dad's standards, of the man's farming abilities. Mom thought well of the wife, who seemed to be a most pleasant person and I believe that Mom sensed that the wife and the son of this man were perhaps fearful of him. I like to think that Mom used her friendship with the mother to monitor the treatment of the boy. I do know that the boy left school and his home to join the military as soon as he could legally do so. Keep in mind, that at this time, the laws were not in place to protect children as they are today. Teachers and schools were not given the services of a child protection agency to report any suspected abuse. Parents took it upon themselves to determine how a child should be treated. Only much later, years later, did I come to believe that the boy who came to school directly from doing his morning chores in the barn was not lazy or unwilling to perform better in school. Rather, I believe that he had been convinced that he could do no better.

One of our teachers was willing and happy to conduct lessons in Industrial Arts. This was actually our arts and crafts class that was held on Fridays. This teacher was always finding projects for children of all ages to get our attention and to develop some creativity in us. The smallest of us would draw, color, finger paint, or construct objects from paper or clay. I remember one time that she acquired some rubber molds so that we could mix Plaster of Paris and pour it into the molds. The Plaster of Paris came in a tub in the form of powder and was measured out and mixed with water. This was poured into the little rubber molds and left to dry, perhaps over the weekend. The molds were then pulled from the hardened forms and could be reused. The next week during class we would be ready to paint our figurines. One of these was of Santa Claus, which many of us chose to make. The girls were encouraged to do some form of working with fabrics. A gift for our mothers, one time, was a handkerchief holder made with pink gingham material and finished on the seams and edges with blanket stitching using embroidery thread. I managed to produce a pot holder that I knitted. It was Mom who provided the lessons for that project. Sometimes we would work with metal. I remember my Mom's getting an aluminum serving tray from one of my brothers for Mothers' Day. The teacher had put a lot of thought into coming up with projects for everyone. I still have a set of bookends that I made from wood, with pictures of roosters on the ends. A paper pattern was laid over the wood piece. Then by following the lines of the picture, a tap of a hammer on the head of a nail along these lines made a permanent impression was left in the wood. I believe that I was in the seventh grade when I was allowed to make a wooden bookcase, my biggest challenge. It involved cutting the wood for three shelves, a plywood back, and a scrolled front at the bottom formed by use of a coping saw. This took some time to finish since I had to sand and stain it when it before it was finished. I suppose all the time I spent out at Dad's workshop gave me some background experience.

We all brought our lunches to school in a lunchbox or sometimes in a brown paper bag. In the cold weather we would eat our lunches at our desks. Mom must have been relieved to get us all out of the house and off to school after packing lunches for 4 every morning I don't know what the normal lunch was for us. I think that the boys usually required 2 sandwiches, whereas all I could eat was one. We always had something sweet in our lunch, like a cookie or a piece of cake. There was usually an apple, an orange or a banana to eat at recess. In the wintertime we enjoyed opening our thermos bottle to find a steamed hotdog to eat or a cup of hot cocoa to drink. Mom would cook our hotdogs in the morning and when they were hot, drop the hotdogs into the thermos bottles where it would stay hot until lunchtime. Other times we would probably have a cold sandwich with a cup of hot cocoa from our thermos. I developed a taste for baked potatoes after bringing a potato to school and letting it bake on top of the stove all morning. Umm, smelling the potatoes baking while we finished our arithmetic or reading lesson is something learned in school that one is not likely to forget! Mom sent salt and pepper and a pat of butter with us to enhance our potatoes. Our teachers were part educators and part mothers. They made sure that we all had our lunches and helped handle the hot potatoes and hot drinks. There were no microwave ovens to nuke our hotdogs or bake our potatoes. There was no instant cocoa mix, but, we were eating tastier lunches than many of the children of today who are eating in the school lunchrooms!

Growing up surrounded by brothers is my excuse for some of my deviltry. I always had to try to stay one step ahead of the next trick or joke to be played on me. My classmate, Janice, had 3 sisters and no brothers, so I guess that's why she was most likely nicer to her friends than I was. She had brought a chicken leg with her to school one day for lunch. She and I were sitting by ourselves out on a grassy bank beside the school house, eating what we had been given by our mothers for lunch. When she brought out the chicken, I told her that I didn't like the leg because of the stringy blood vein, and was quick to point it out to her. Needless to say, she didn't finish her chicken that day and I don't remember her bringing chicken with her any time after that. Now, that was just plain mean, I know. But at the time I didn't consider it as being mean. We did things like that to each other all of the time with our siblings.

We had a dog who treated us like a nanny may have. He would

accompany us to school every morning and as soon as we went indoors, he would trot back to the house. But, he would be back as soon as he heard our voices at recess to play with us and to be fondled by everyone on the playground. He would go home and reappear when we were outside. Finally, at 4 o'clock every afternoon, he would be waiting outside the door at school to usher us back home. We didn't have a lamb like Mary to follow us to school, but we had something better!

A little boy in Lois' class lived a mile from school, another half a mile further than us. Arlen was the oldest child in his family. His little brother was just a baby when he entered the first grade. Arlen's mother would drive him to school every morning and make sure that the teacher had her eyes on him as she left him. However, during recess, Arlen would hide rather than return to the classroom. The windbreak around the school provided a number of good limbs in the trees where little boys could climb. As soon as everyone knew his hiding place, Arlen would find a new tree. He never seemed to tire of escaping. If his mother wasn't at the school at the minute school let out, he would run across the field to our apple orchard and hide from her there. It soon became a regular routine for his mother. If he didn't come home after school, she would go to the school to pick him up. If she missed him there, she would stop at our house and call him. If he failed to show up or answer her call, we would be enlisted to check the branches of the apple trees and bring him down. 'Just wanted to get an apple' was his excuse. Other times he would hide in the barn or one of the other buildings. He moved with his family from our neighborhood shortly after he had started school. I have wondered at times what might have happened to him and where his rampant ambition may have taken him in life.

Summers with Aunt Hannah
An Only Child for a Week

W hen I was between six and eight years of age it was during the time that our family lived in the little house. I spent a week or two with my mother's sister, Hannah, and her family on their farm. I have wondered in recent years whether I was sent there because I asked to go, if Hannah asked for me to visit, or if the house we lived in was so crowded that everyone benefited from my absence. At any rate, I felt special being the only child in a house with grown people. My cousin, Twyla, was home from college for the summer and she shared her bedroom with me and let me borrow her pens and paper. She also took me shopping and bought me new summer sandals, something I would probably not have gotten at home.

My mother's sisters all had individual talents of which to be especially proud. Aunt Sina, for example, was the master of crocheting and made everything from doilies to beautiful bedspreads. Aunt Hannah was the recycling champion. She not only produced countless quilts from new and used materials, but she had a great number of braided rag rugs. The rugs were made from strips of material from old wool clothing and denim overalls. The one I remember seeing was the oval one in the big bedroom that I shared with Twyla. It covered a large portion of the hardwood floor in the room.

They lived on a farm with two houses, the old house and the new house. This is what they called them. The old house was the original house that they had lived in before they built a more modern house next to it. The old house was used as the garage for their car and for storage. Later, Uncle Clarence used it as a shop where he restored old cars. Uncle Clarence was a mechanical genius. He would go to junkyards to find parts for his old car restoration projects and come back with what was needed to get the machine running. He didn't stop with the mechanics. He worked to make those old Model T Fords look like new! He made his own riding lawn mower before riding mowers were being marketed. He accomplished all of this in spite of a severe limp that he had from childhood, when he fell from a horse and broke his hip. Without proper setting, he was left with a limp for the rest of his life.

Naturally, as a youngster accustomed to running free on the farm, I came face to face with their mad rooster. He didn't like anybody getting around his hen house, I guess. I caught on in a hurry not to venture into that rooster's domain again. I did go into the big white barn where I visited with Maude, their old mare and went with Aunt Hannah while she milked the cow. She brought the milk to the house and strained and refrigerated it. I'm sure she didn't do this every day, but only when milk was needed. The other cows were milked by Ole, their hired hand. Aunt Hannah wanted to make sure that the milk that they drank was clean, so she took that task on herself, winter and summer. I should mention that Aunt Hannah was somewhat of a hypochondriac and a germophobic.

Aunt Hannah had a flower garden where I remember she always had sweet peas that she brought in to put in a vase on the kitchen table. They, of course, also had a vegetable garden, but I don't remember her being out there. I seem to recall that Ole did the weeding and maybe Hannah did the picking.

I was introduced to bubble gum when I was visiting there. Some friends or relatives came out to visit them from Minneapolis and their children had bubble gum that they shared with me. I went home to demonstrate my ability to blow bubbles, but that wasn't received nearly as well as I had hoped. Bubble gum would be banned from the house for all time. Dad didn't approve of chewing gum and wouldn't let us have gum in our mouths in his presence. He labeled it nasty.

I managed to be at Aunt Hannah's house the week that the local country church was having Vacation Bible School. Neighbors of theirs, who also happened to be relatives, would pick me up on their way and drop me off at the end of the driveway on the their way home at noon. This worked out well, except the day that I couldn't get to the house before I felt an urgent need to use the bathroom. I did what kids do in the country when they are too far from a bathroom. I stepped from the driveway into the wood next to the road where I wouldn't be seen. Unfortunately, by the time I did get to the house, I realized that my stop in the woods was in the middle of a poison ivy patch. Thankfully, Aunt Hannah had Calamine lotion and I found out what a wonderful medicine that was!

Aunt Hannah, like my mother, played the piano. Uncle Clarence played the violin. They would play duets at home and occasionally they could be persuaded to play at church. Is it any wonder that I enjoyed visiting with them?

The house had some unique things about it that fascinated me at the time. They seemed to always have a big cured dried beef shoulder hanging in the basement stairwell. It smelled so good and made a delicious sandwich to go with a glass of lemonade. They also had a laundry chute going to the basement. A little door in the second floor bathroom allowed dirty linens and clothes to get to the washing machine with ease. We didn't have that luxury at home. It just didn't take much to impress a little country girl!

FAMILY EXCURSIONS
Taking the Show on the Road

Although most of the family outings involved getting together with my Mom's and Dad's family, other times we visited with other friends and neighbors. One time, the Barnum and Bailey Circus was appearing in Watertown, South Dakota. We left early in the morning with picnic lunches and joined another family there to spend the day at the circus. As so often happens, the circus got to the fairgrounds later than expected, so as a result we witnessed the circus workers raising the big top as we anticipated getting in to see the Greatest Show on Earth. I remember that the prairie wind was blowing dust into our picnic lunches. We were all sitting on the grass drinking warm lemonade and getting pretty hot while the grit was settling in our hair and darkening our faces. But, it was exciting to see and hear the elephants working to help erect the tents. The big cats could be heard roaring in their cages as our excitement intensified. When we finally got into the big tent, it was almost anticlimactic after our behind the scenes view of the readying for the event. I do remember an amazing show of trapeze artists and the lion tamer. Of course, we all laughed at all of the clowns pouring out of the little car. I do know that we were a tired bunch when we got home that night and washed the dirt and circus smells from our bodies.

There is a town named Clear Lake, in South Dakota, where rodeos were held in a natural amphitheater. We went to watch the bronco and bull riding, barrel racing, and calf roping. Loud speakers announced the name of the rider and the name of the wild bronco he

107

rode as they came out of the chute. Soon the announcer would call out the time spent in the saddle. The bull riding competition was a favorite. The rider hung on for dear life while the bull tried his best to shake the man off. When the rider lost his grip the clowns would come out into the ring to distract the bull from the thrown cowboy. As the clown darted behind the barrels for protection, he waited for the right moment to run for the fence. At this time the cowboys on horses would gallop in and herd the bull back to the holding pen. Roping calves from the back of a horse at a full gallop gave all the boys an example of a skill to practice at home. (Nobody ever warned us to "not to try this at home.") Once again, we managed to get dusty and very sunburned sitting on the side of the hill overlooking the corral down below. I remember always being glad to get back home after a long day, but thankful for the memories which were relived for days afterward.

I don't remember exactly when the family took several days off from the farm to visit the Black Hills and Mount Rushmore. I think that I was around twelve years old when we all piled into the family car and headed west to see the Badlands of South Dakota. We did most of the tourist things. We visited Wall Drugs, which was a big disappointment after seeing all of the signs that followed Highway 212 all the way across the two states. It turned out to be nothing but a big souvenir store and restaurant with stuffed buffalo and deer heads hanging on the walls. But, after all of the invitations issued on the roadside signs, we had to stop and check the place out. I do note that we could take in all that we could with our eyes, but we didn't spend a lot of our spending money on worthless junk souvenirs.

At that time, the accommodations for sleeping were less than luxurious and hardly comfortable. There were not many motels at the time. Most of the resting places for tourists were cabins appropriately called tourist cabins. The cabin that we stayed in had a kerosene stove for cooking where Mom cooked a lot of the food that we ate while we were there. To be honest, we probably ate better than many others who ate their meals in restaurants. The highlight of the whole trip, I think, was seeing The Passion Play near Spearfish, South Dakota, one evening. It was set outdoors in a natural amphitheater, once again, but this time we sat on wooden bleachers. Naturally, a must see was

Mount Rushmore. We marveled at the sight along with everyone else and speculated on how such a feat could be accomplished at such a height.

There was only one other actual family vacation that we took. Once again, we packed out bags and headed out, first to Duluth to see the shipping docks at Lake Superior. It was exciting to see the ocean liners at the dock in Minnesota, and it was the next best thing to seeing a real ocean. Really, the deep water right at the shore's edge, and not being able to see the opposite shore, put it right up there with seeing the Atlantic Ocean for the first time.

Leaving Duluth, we headed still further north to the Iron Range and drove past the open iron ore mines near Virginia, Minnesota. The terrain of Minnesota in the northern part of the state was very different from the grasslands of the southern end. We saw a lot of pine trees and countless lakes. We had the thrill of seeing the Mississippi River headwaters and walked across the stones at the river's northernmost point. On a visit to Lake Itaska recently, it was obvious that times have changed. What I had remembered as a simple sign marking the origin of the great Mississippi now boasts a well-groomed visitors center and souvenir shop. I'm glad that I saw it in the rough and natural when I was little.

We couldn't come that close to Bemidji and not pause to see the home of Paul Bunyon and his Blue Ox. A statue had been erected in their honor. We had read the stories about Paul and his Blue Ox and their amazing feats. I think all children should be encouraged to read these stories. We spent the night in Bemidji in another one of those tourist cabins. This time the cabin happened to be next to a railroad track, which shook us awake every time a train came through, or we may have already been awakened by the train whistle blowing next to our heads.

Our excursion included a visit to Dad's Uncle Lars, Grandpa's brother, where we spent the night with him and his wife, Bertha. Uncle Lars was also a Norwegian immigrant who settled farther to the north. As a consequence of the distance and the time, we didn't get to see these relatives often. I know my Dad really enjoyed the visit. I can still picture the two of them sitting out under the trees in Lars' front yard. After resting there, we headed south and home to our normal farm life. I would like to note that these long automobile rides were in the family car, not an SUV, and there was no air conditioning. Most of us, now, would not dream of driving that distance in the heat of the summer, where the only air stirring would be from the open windows of the car. We must have all been hot and windblown, not to mention dirty! Indeed, it was a different, but memorable, time.

There were, oh, so many Sunday afternoon drives. We would start out all excited about going somewhere unknown to us kids. Sometimes, I'm sure, Dad and Mom really didn't have a plan, other times they would surprise us with a visit to the home of an aunt and uncle or grandparents. When we were all quite small it was a little crowded with all of us in the family sedan. This was before the introduction of seatbelts, so we would flop about in the back seat, sometimes trading places. Everyone wanted a seat by the window, but needless to say, with four or five of us in the back seat, there weren't enough windows to go around. Paul would often climb up to the rear window and sprawl out until he outgrew the space. The youngest, Lois, would usually be in the front seat between Mom and Dad while the rest of us in back tried to keep our disagreements quiet enough so we weren't told that we were going to have to turn around and go home because of our bad behavior! I don't think we ever actually went home without the Sunday outing, but the warning kept us in line.

These rides served the purpose for my Dad of checking on the crops in other farmers' fields, judging whether or not they were getting as much or more rain than our farm had gotten, or to see who was behind on the planting, cultivating or picking. I think that usually Dad would get back home pleased with himself for his farming expertise.

One afternoon, we were treated to a visit to the farm of a former neighbor whose grown sons had acquired a two-seater airplane. We had been invited to come out to their field-turned runway to take a ride above the old neighborhood. This was the first plane ride for all of us and the only one my dad would ever take. We flew over the homes of the people we knew and followed the river and roads. This was something we talked about for a long time and only one of us became ill. Of course, it was Paul, the bravest one of us all who got sick. Even in his adult years, he would drive long distances in preference to flying.

On several different occasions Mom would take us with her to pick gooseberries out by the river. She would make jelly and other preserves from them. One of the favorite desserts that we would have in the evenings throughout the week would be some fruit brought from the basement shelves in a jar. The fruit might be apples, peaches, pears, raspberries, strawberries, gooseberries or any other type of fruit that my mother might get her hands on. The fruit had been cooked in a syrup (sugar and water) and canned and sealed in jars. Gooseberry picking was an afternoon adventure, since the spot that had an abundance of berries was next to an old, nearly forgotten, and out of the way cemetery. The markers that were still visible had the names of the deceased and the dates of their births and deaths. We soon recognized that people of all ages had died within a very short time span. Many of the dead buried here were babies and old people. Later we learned that a settlement that had been in that area had been abandoned after a large number had died from a fever. I'm not entirely sure, but I think it was typhoid fever. Once again, we are reminded of the extreme hardships and sadness that the early settlers had to endure. The cemetery is less than a mile from the birthplace of my Dad. The last time I visited that cemetery the site had been restored to some extent after vandals had been there and trashed some of the markers. A fence had been put around the burial plots, giving a sense of dignity to the spot.

City Cousin Lovin' the Country
Baby Pigs Are the Cutest!

My mother's parents raised six children who were born over an 18-year period. My mother, being the youngest, had several nieces and nephews who were close to her in age. Furthermore, since my parents didn't marry and start their family until they were both 30, several of my cousins had children the same age as me.

One of my cousins, Glenn, had a daughter who was just two months older than me. This was Sally, whose name of record was Solveigh, and who for a short period of time, decided that she wanted to be called Sophie. She and I grew up together and shared not only family, but school and church and were almost like sisters throughout our childhood. We performed duets in Sunday School when we were in first grade, she with the long dark brown hair and me with the long blonde braids. We were flower girls in my cousins' wedding in matching pink gowns that her mother made for us.

She was born with one leg shorter than the other and even after surgery always had a limp. This she more than compensated for with a bubbly personality and a fearlessness that often amazed me. She loved animals and had everything her parents would allow. This included a pair of hamsters (big mistake) that quickly became a village of little hamsters, and a dog and a number of cats, one at a time. Her dad had a weakness for dogs, himself, and brought home an Airedale he named Dexter. Since he didn't have any sons, he referred to Dexter as his boy and treated him like a prince, even feeding him a piece of his steak! I remember thinking how great it was to allow your dog to be in the house and sit beside the table while we ate. Things like that didn't happen on the farm.

I often envied Sally her city surroundings where friends might live next door, where one could walk down the sidewalk just a couple of blocks and buy an ice cream cone at the cafe or drop in at her Grandpa's and Dad's store to beg a nickel for a pack of gum. Town was where you could go to an afternoon matinee at the movie theatre and not have to wait for parents to have the time to drive you there. There were sidewalks where you could roller skate and streets where you could ride your bike without having to watch out for rocks in the road.

I soon discovered that Sally envied me as much or more for the privilege of living on the farm and coming in from play with dirt on our clothes, and, on occasion, manure on our shoes. She itched to pick up a new-born piglet and hold him under her chin. She didn't even seem to mind the mess he left on her white blouse. I think she may have hugged him just a little too tight.

Her mom and dad came to expect that she would go back home with a piece of the farm attached to her shoes and the back of her jeans. But, one thing that she did which got a thumbs down from her dad was the evening that he came to take her home and she was a little too eager to get into the car with an old coffee can in her hands. His suspicions were confirmed when Sally was questioned about the contents of the can and she revealed a nest of pink baby field mice found out in the woods. We had to take them 'back to their mother' in the woods before she was allowed to get into the car. Really, they didn't look much different from the baby hamsters that she had at home.

As we grew older, we found excitement in challenging our parents' ability to control us. Several times I was given permission to spend a night with Sally on some excuse or another. Sally asked me just a few years ago during a telephone conversation if I thought she had gotten me into trouble. I had never considered that possibility before she mentioned it. Of course, I responded that I didn't feel that she had been a bad influence. Yet, now, I realize that without a friend like Sally, I would never have done some of the things that I did.

I secretly resented Dave for scaring me half to death when driving to school on the gravel roads at seemingly break-neck speeds. Sally helped me get even with him one evening when we spotted the pickup truck parked on main street outside one of the cafes. We crawled up into the bed of the truck and hunkered down to surprise him. It wasn't long before he came back to the truck with his girlfriend and surprisingly, neither one of them noticed the passengers in the back. When they went out onto one of the country roads outside of town, I think we began to realize that we had remained quiet for too long. We proceeded to make noise. This was not a good idea as it turned out. Dave took off like a shot back to the street lights of downtown. To say that he was surprised and more than a little upset is probably an understatement. I find it hard to believe him when he tells me that he doesn't remember that night!

Of course, Sally and I weren't always looking for trouble or something to get into. There were youth church meetings, wiener roasts with other friends down at the river and school dances after the basketball games in the gym. I guess these were called sock hops since we weren't allowed on the gym floor with our shoes on at the dances.

Sally liked to read magazines focusing on crime stories and, for a short time, had me interested in reading about the daring escapades of thieves and murderers. Sally showed me how we could raise the window in her bedroom and push out the storm glass. Anticipating what the answer would be if we asked her mother if we could go out after dark one winter night, we tried the escape route. From the window sill it was a short drop to the walkway outside her bedroom window. The only thing we did was walk the two or three blocks from her house to downtown and roam about for an hour or so. Then we came back to her house and making sure everyone was in bed, let ourselves in the door with a key. We simply left the house in an unconventional way and left without asking permission.

Other times we would hang out in her room and paint our fingernails and listen to LP records on her phonograph. One time, we decided to see what we would look like if she were blonde and I was a brunette. We struggled all afternoon to try to get my hair colored dark brown. Since we really didn't know what we were doing, my hair turned into a charcoal gray. Sally chickened out on trying to bleach her hair and simply put on a hair scarf with a tuft of blonde wig sticking out like bangs in the front. Mom and Dad were not happy with the experiment. It took a lot of shampoo over the next two days to get my hair color back to normal.

The biggest mistake we made, and the last adventure we would have as teenagers, was the afternoon in the spring that was too nice a day to go back to school after lunch. The whole scheme centered around the fact that Sally's dad and grandfather had gone to a furniture convention or something in Minneapolis. The old Kaiser automobile belonging to Sally's grandpa, my Uncle Johnny, was parked in front of Sally's house. I was invited to have lunch with Sally and her mother that day before we were to head back to school. Sally asked her mother's permission to drive the old car back to school, and miraculously, permission was given. It didn't take long to find the street out of town. What a thrill to have the afternoon to do as we pleased. After all, no one had any idea where we were. We simply spent the afternoon driving around, seeing a neighboring town or two before heading back to Sally's with the car to coincide with the time that school was out. This also was the time that the principal and of some of his teacher friends were walking down to a cafe for coffee and happened to see us driving proudly down the main street. The next morning we both returned to our regular classes to be told to report to the assembly hall and take seats. We spent the entire day in study hall as the teachers were giving us zeros for the day. Only later did we find out that our parents had been called when we failed to return from lunch the previous day and that a decision had been made to give us the silent treatment, fearing that a confrontation might have resulted in our dropping out of school. Little did they know that neither one of us would have done anything that drastic. We were, after all, a couple of pretty good kids!

Much too soon, we became old enough to drive back and forth to each others' homes, but at the same time we were so busy with more important things that we stopped playing with baby chicks and pigs. Isn't it odd how the details of the days when we were little are so much more vivid and treasured than the memories of the all important teenage years?

Sadly, Sally died two years ago before we really had the opportunity to relive some of our childhood frolics. We talked long distance a number of times over the last few years after a long period of silence. I was naïve enough to believe that there was plenty of time to reminisce in the time to come. Here again, "too soon old, too late smart."

$\sim\!\!\diamond\!\!\sim$

THOSE AWKWARD 'TWEEN YEARS
Just Waiting to Grow Up

$\sim\!\!\diamond\!\!\sim$

Sometime between those years of being reminded regularly by my older brothers that I was different from them (being a girl) and being reminded by my mother to act like a lady, I had a lot of adjusting of my own to do before I fit into the 'teenage girl' mold. Branching out into familiar places with a new view of the rest of the world is just a step in growing up. I found myself gradually being trusted to move about independently of family members. That can be freeing and, at the same time, scary. There was much to be learned in a short period of time before becoming an adult. The most difficult time, I think, is those 'tween years' as they call them. Not babies, and not yet teens. Anybody who says they never felt awkward at this period of their life is lying.

Living in a small town, most of the store owners and workers know all of the teenagers in town, or, if not the young people, they know their parents. I had favorite places to visit. First of all places was the furniture store. Mom frequently stopped in just to say hello to her brother, Rob. She would buy liquid furniture polish from him. They bought polish in large containers that they would use on the furniture in the store, but would also sell the polish in small bottles to anyone who asked. The polish was put into empty bottles that had previously contained embalming fluid. I found this to be a fact after asking Mom why the furniture bottle never had a manufacturer's label on it. The furniture store building also housed the mortuary at the rear. When Sally and I were just big enough to be curious about the undertaking business we would slip into the back room where the dead had been prepared for burial. Sally always knew when they had a body and we would check to see if the coffin was open when we were there. I guess this just satisfied our morbid curiosity. There was not a lot of excitement to be had, so this was another attempt at livening things up a little!

I remember frequent overnight stays with my best friend, Sally, sneaking out at night to go downtown to see if anyone else was out– someone was always out! After choir practice on Wednesday nights we would go to one of the cafes downtown and have hot chocolate or cokes, depending on the season, and ice cream sandwiches, play the jukebox and wish we wouldn't have to go home so early and get up for school the next day.

A favorite place for all of us kids was the drugstore where we went to get our prescriptions filled, although needing a prescription medication didn't happen that often. Our doctors didn't demand to see us unless we had a problem and asked to see them. The Doctors Johnson, H.M. and Bill, and Doctor Boody managed to see to our ailments and kept us all pretty healthy. The drugstore in town didn't have the ice cream, soda fountain or lunch counter the way that the bigger drugstores in bigger cities did, but they had a good selection of candy bars when the cost of most was a mere nickel. The big Nut Goody was a dime. This was the only place in town where you could buy a magazine, or, in the case of my brothers, a comic book. Trading comic books was a favorite pastime for my brothers and their friends. I bought my first lipstick in Hovland's Drugstore and smelled the perfume samples on the counter.

I remember going along on a trip to town with my mother. David couldn't or didn't want to go along, but he was almost out of rifle shells. I was probably ten or twelve at the time and with his dollar in hand, I went into the hardware store where they knew us and bought a box of 22 longs.

The one time that I shot a gun that wasn't just target practice was the time when I picked up a rifle from back porch where it was kept and walked out into the grove of trees that surround the farm build-ings. I spotted a squirrel high up in a tree overhead and, without giv-ing it a second thought, aimed and fired, killing the squirrel. It totally surprised me to realize that the first shot had killed the creature. That was the first and last time that I remember killing anything with a gun.

With getting older comes responsibility. This includes chores that were considered dangerous for young children, and also learning to keep some of the new-found knowledge to oneself. My mother was most respectful of fire. This is understandable, since she had escaped a house fire. We knew she meant it when she told us to stay away from a hot stove and never to play with matches. I won her trust to handle hot things when I was maybe 12 years old. Mom had errands to take care of in town and also had bread rising in pans waiting to go into the oven. She told me how to decide when the bread had risen enough and what temperature the oven should be when the bread was to go into the oven. With those instructions to me, she left and I successfully baked the bread and, when the allotted time had passed, took the loaves out of the oven and turned them out to cool. Success! Mom probably thought about her bread the whole time she was gone, wondering if I had remembered all of the things that she had told me. I suspect that I already had a pretty good idea of the process after watching her do it so many times. Mom would bake five loaves of bread twice a week. Dad had made it plain that he didn't like the bread that was in the stores. So, we were never without homemade bread. Baking bread is still a satisfying and rewarding task. Melting butter on warm bread smells and tastes like a little piece of childhood to me.

Sometime in the late forties or early fifties, margarine was introduced to our farm community. The dairy industry had pretty much succeeded in having the sale of the butter substitute outlawed in Minnesota and Wisconsin. At this time, Iowa had lifted their ban on margarine and it was available there in its natural white form. However the plastic bag container came with a capsule of yellow coloring so the consumer could mix the color into the white mass. This made the margarine (oleo) look like butter. There was such a demand for this 'new butter' that some individuals (housewives) drove across the state line into Iowa to bring the bootleg margarine back for themselves and friends. I can remember only one time that this product made it into our home, although it may have been on the table more times when I was not aware of its identity.

My cousin, Glenn, joined the furniture business with his father and uncle, and, I believe did much of the buying for the store. He attended the conventions where manufacturers would display their new merchandise. He was several years younger than Mom when she lived in the house with him and his parents, her sister and brother-in-law, Nora and Johnny. My mother told of a time when Nora and Johnny had gone somewhere and had left Glenn under the watchful eye of my mother. During his parents' absence, Glenn tried his hand at making wine from some available berries. What I remember hearing is that the wine was considered a successful endeavor, but the excessive tasting resulted in a very sick wine maker. Mom told of how angry she was with Glenn who had stepped out of line under her supervision. He became a responsible family man, but being his mother's only son, he was very close to both of his parents. After his dad died, he would regularly go to his mother's house to join her for lunch at noon. Being raised in a small town complicates relationships and loyalties.

TEENAGE YEARS IN THE FIFTIES
True, You Can't Go Back in Time

❧

We had no television until I was a teenager. The reception was very poor at first. One of the television stations that we received from was in Alexandria, Minnesota and another was in Watertown, South Dakota. Of course, everything was in black and white in the beginning and there was a lot of local advertising. At that time most of the shows were variety shows, like *Bob Hope*, *The Honeymooners* (with Jackie Gleason and Audrey Meadows), *American Bandstand* and *Lawrence Welk*. There was also *Wagon Train* and *Gunsmoke*, *The Jimmy Dean Show* and a host of others. Most of the entertainment programs were a half hour long and news broadcasts were fifteen minutes to begin with. My mother was delighted when the soap operas began to be televised. She would allow herself to watch just one of the shows every afternoon. I never knew her to stop her work to listen to the soaps on the radio, but televised soaps demanded that she sit down and watch!

Television or not, bedtime was nine o'clock for the farm family. Lights were out and everyone to their bedroom. Many times I would read after going to bed and many times my mother would make rounds and turn out my bedside light after I had fallen asleep with a book in my hand. I still can't stay awake to read in bed.

When I entered my teen years, I discovered the Carnegie library for the first time. When I was younger, the teacher would make a trip to the library for us and bring back the books we requested or she would pick out a couple of books that she thought we would like.

Going to the library and finding all of the books at our disposal was fabulous. Nothing, absolutely nothing, smells as good as a library. I remember how much fun I had picking out novels like *Girl of the Limberlost* and realizing that poetry and plays were enjoyable when they were of your own choosing. The school had a library and provided another source of reading materials. There I experienced the excitement of psychology and biographies, cashing in on the chance to examine other peoples' lives and to marvel at them.

There is probably nothing as hard, or as much fun and rewarding, as living on a farm in the Midwest growing up. We were raised at a time that will never be experienced again. We thought we were deprived a lot of times, I guess. We all had friends who didn't have chores to do before they left for school in the morning. We had friends who lived in town and didn't have to catch a school bus and go straight home from school, but could meander around downtown or visit with one another, do homework with a friend or go to the library. On the other hand, looking back I realize that some of our friends had to go home and pitch in because their mothers worked outside of the home and didn't get the amount of attention that we got every day. Maybe we were, in fact, the lucky ones.

Somehow, we survived without so much as a broken bone. We escaped the polio epidemic and all of the other dangers around. I had to have my tonsillectomy delayed until the following summer, following a severe infection. I ended up in the hospital for a week taking penicillin every three hours, day and night. There were no surgeries being done, other than emergencies due to a polio epidemic breaking out all across the country. We did eventually all have our tonsils removed. Dave and I had ours out the same day, Roger alone, and Paul and Lois went in together. We had the usual childhood diseases: mumps, chicken pox and of course, measles. We had our share of bruises and scrapes and close calls, but we all came through it all without too many hangups or long lasting disagreements.

Picture, if you can, a sleepy little town with just a little over a thousand people living in it. Imagine a town surrounded by farmland on all sides, with the main street running north and south from the highway on the north end, a boulevard running down the middle until you came to the railroad tracks. There the business district began on the other side of the tracks. There was the post office, three grocery stores competing with each other on friendly terms, a dime store, two drugstores, a bakery with the aroma of fresh bread wafting out the door, three cafes, a men's clothing store and a women's clothing store (both locally owned), and a furniture store. Included in this string of three blocks were two banks (at least for a time), a hotel, a barber shop, a beauty shop and a couple of beer joints. We mustn't forget the movie theatre and, of course the National Guard Armory on one of the side streets across from the library. Parking was available on main street; diagonal parking, of course, and also parallel parking on the side streets. If you preferred, you could park in the alley behind the Red Owl Grocery store and run in through the back door to pick up a couple of things if you were in a hurry. Those were the days when a family member could go in to get some much needed items and sign the receipt (hand-written, no less) to be paid for later in the week when we brought in maybe twelve dozen eggs to be sold at the hatchery on the street behind Main for cash. Or maybe Mom would write a check for what was owed even though the checking account only had Dad's name on it. Later Mom was told when she visited the bank that she shouldn't be signing her name to the checks, so she began signing Dad's name instead. This was okay. The auditors were checking for correct signatures, not forged ones, I guess.

At the south end of the main street was a gas station on one side of the street and on the other side of the street was a small church. The town didn't lack for churches. There were two Lutheran churches, a Presbyterian church, a Catholic church and a Pentecostal church scattered throughout town. Then we came to a small park by the Lac qui Parle River. This was one of two municipal parks. The other park was on the other end of town by the highway on the eastern end. This one had a swimming park and playground equipment built by the CWA, the Civil Works Administration, during the depression in the thirties. On the western end of town, next to the highway, was the golf course. What could possibly be missing in this town that the average person might need?

I recall the excitement that was generated when the drive-in movie theatre came to the community! The screen went up a few miles outside of town just off the highway. Admission was charged by the number of occupants in the car. I don't remember what the admission charge was, probably very little, but that didn't prevent teenagers from cheating the establishment by bringing one of movie-goers in the trunk of the car as they drove by the ticket window. I understand that this was a common occurrence and that some of the drive-ins even performed searches of the vehicles with teen drivers. I was told that one of my brothers was a party to such a scheme but, of course, this was only a rumor. Drive-in theaters were a far cry from being a fine art form, but more of an opportunity for a series of small parties during the warm summer months. Winter closed down the theatres and snow covered the parking places with the sound speakers sticking up in the air like a memorial park.

Back at home, changes on the farm seemed to be gradual, but young people usually aren't involved in the business end of farming, especially if you happen to be a teenage girl. Some things, of course, are subjects of discussion at the supper table. Dad was visibly upset one evening, when he told us about some pheasant hunters he had met that day. Actually, he had a little run-in with a couple of *gun-carrying city slickers*. Dad had taken the time to go out to buy some No Hunting signs in town and had gone around the perimeter of the farm, nailing the signs to telephone poles. To set foot on our farm was a serious offense to the landowner. First of all, the corn was still in the fields and was ready to be picked and anyone who walked through the field would likely knock the corn ears off the stalks to lay on the ground after the harvest. Secondly, Dad was out in the field on the tractor with the corn picker at the time and really didn't want to be in the line of fire between the hunters and the pheasants. An incidental, third reason may have been that Dad and my brothers may well have wanted to bag those birds themselves. I don't think that Dad would have been angry if the hunters had walked back to their car and driven away after being asked to do so. What upset Dad was the fact that when he made the turn in the field to come back in their direction, the hunters were still tromping through the field, knocking corn down, trying to spot pheasants before they left.

One summer when I was a teenager, Mom was away for a couple of days for some reason, probably visiting my brother's family. Dad came up to my bedroom early in the morning where Sally was spending the night with me. To wake up with Dad at the door of my bedroom surprised me as that had never happened before. When he asked me if I could make dinner for the balers, he caught me off guard. He said he could take them into town and feed them at a restaurant if I couldn't handle it. I took the challenge and told him I could cook a meal. I had never attempted anything like that before. But, I had watched Mom prepare thousands of meals and how hard could that be? She made it look so easy! I also thought that Sally could help me, but she was not that confident and she had her dad pick her up that morning to take her home. So, having committed to cooking for four or five hungry men, I went down to the freezer and took out some packages of round steak to thaw. Next, I brought up a generous number of potatoes, which I peeled and cooked. I fried steak, made gravy and heated some canned vegetables from the garden. Mom always had a supply of loaves of bread that she had baked so we had a meal! The guests said the food was good and I had no reason to believe otherwise. Most importantly, Dad said that I had performed well, which was all I really cared about. My memories are that of me standing at the stove, anxious for everything to be done on time. On the farm, dinner is at noon on the dot!

Sometime during those years the transition was made from hands-on to automated milking. As the farm operation grew and the number of cows increased, milking machines were introduced and large refrigerators were installed in the milk room. Where once a cream separator held a prominent place in the room, now big cans of raw milk were stored in the refrigerator to wait for the dairy truck to arrive. The milk was delivered to the creamery where it would be pasteurized and homogenized and handled according to government regulations. Farming was becoming big business.

It wouldn't seem as though there could possibly be any time in our busy young lives to get into any trouble. We attended confirmation instruction every Saturday morning, nine months out of the year, for two years in junior and senior classes. At the end of the second year, in May, we would be confirmed in the Lutheran church and receive our first communion. We would be quizzed by the pastor at that time, to ensure the members of the congregation that we understood the teachings of the Bible from our attendance as children in the church. We all stood proudly at the front of the church in white gowns, ready for high school and the world beyond!

From this time on we were invited to join the senior members of choir in church. Choir practice was held on Wednesday evening and high school members of the choir would often go downtown to Tommy's Cafe and treat ourselves to cokes or ice cream sandwiches. My favorite was, and still is today, brownies and vanilla ice cream. If we hadn't had enough music, someone always had a nickel for the jukebox. Rock 'n roll had entered our world and our parents hoped and prayed that that fad would be short-lived.

We roamed the downtown streets and stores to stay in touch with the pulse of the community. But, we soon discovered that there was more out there on the other side of the city limits and our own farm homes. We became acquainted with kids from neighboring towns and an out-of-town car would be seen cruising main street from time to time. Their visits would be reciprocated with a tour through their town by our friendly representatives. If we felt an urge to go bowling, we had to go to Montevideo. Movies came to the larger town before ours, giving us an excuse to further our horizons a little more. We would go by car or by school bus to witness the football and basket-ball games in surrounding towns. The trip in itself was pure joy and a winning match only added icing to the cake. Did we ever have arguments or disagreements about anything? I don't remember anything like that, but then again hurt feelings and bad times must, over time, take a back seat to the happy times. I have no memories of regrettable times, although surely there had to have been times that were not so sweet.

HIGH SCHOOL DAYS
The Good, the Bad and the Required

I remember looking forward to entering high school after seeing my older brothers take that step before me. It seemed like it would be an exciting time and a huge step in growing up.

As it turned out, I left the one-room schoolhouse in the second year of junior high. There had been just myself and one other girl in the seventh grade and *the powers that must have been* decided we should begin the eighth grade in town. So, the transition was a year earlier than expected. Going from a school with one room, providing an education to 8 grades simultaneously, to a school of several rooms for each grade, was exciting and just a little intimidating. Getting a hall locker and finding the way between classes is something that all kids experience, but it seemed like an adventure to me.

After adjusting to the routine of being in Junior High, I began to form opinions of likes and dislikes. This included the subject material and the teachers. A great many of the teachers and staff who were in this small town school came to stay. There must have been something about the town to keep so many of them there for so long. Obviously, the small town atmosphere suits some people more than others. In addition to that, the people who made up the population had to make their decision to stay an easier one. After all, this small town in the Midwest was a safe place to live and raise children. Teachers with families joined the community churches and activities. Some of the teachers took summer jobs to supplement their salaries. As an example, I remember one of the high school faculty worked at the park in the summertime. Many of the elementary school teachers were women, wives of businessmen in town. This family type of involvement added to the familiarity within the community.

I decided that I really didn't like PE (physical education). I didn't much like the girls' PE teacher or the curriculum. Girls athletics were still a thing of the future in schools then. If we had had some serious competitive sports for girls I think that we would have had a lot more fun! I pretty much finished that course of study after I made a bad landing doing a flip and cracked my pelvis. I thought I was all right until the shooting pains started shortly after I had gotten into my next class, Social Studies. I went down to the school office where I insisted that they get my brother, Dave, out of class so he could take me home. Of course, Mom took me to the doctor where an X-ray showed the crack. This earned me a couple of weeks of bed rest at home until the injury healed. The doctor's note exempted me from activity until the PE requirement was over.

The first year or more that I was in school here, phys ed classes were held in the National Guard Armory. There could not have been a more uninviting shower room than the one that we had. It was designed for military use with the community showers and the institutional green paint everywhere. Construction had begun, while I was still in Junior High, on a large addition to the school. The addition included additional elementary classrooms, a band room and of course the auditorium where we finally had a basketball court on the premises and a place for all of the other extra-curricular activities. Up until this time, the high school basketball practices and games took place in the armory. For the first time we had an arena for lyceum programs that provided entertainment and education. We had class plays, band and choir concerts here, along with school dances and graduations.

My other least favorite class was Home Economics. Our teacher was young, but had strict old-fashioned ideas. She demanded that we come to her class with a skirt on, even on casual Friday. So we would dash to our lockers to replace our slacks or blue jeans with a skirt until that class was over. Most of us girls kept a skirt in our locker, which we didn't really care about, that we would use just for this purpose, to please our Home Ec teacher. After class we would run back to our lockers to put on our jeans. I hated the sewing portion of the class. Mom had taught me how to sew and I thought that I knew enough of the basics without a class. I guess the point I make is that I just didn't enjoy sewing that much.

There was a teacher for a couple years at the school who was the librarian and also the French teacher. Her name was Miss DeGroot. I didn't take French, but had contact with her in the library. She seemed as out of place as a duck out of water and kids would ridicule her behind her back. Being a lady, she wore dresses every day, but apparently she didn't take kindly to the frigid temperatures of the winters, and she would cope with the decision of being a lady vs. being cold in her own way. It didn't take long for us to realize that the poor woman was wearing two pair of nylon stockings in an attempt to stay warm. It was obvious that she wore two pairs since the seams in the back of her legs created two lines (crooked) and her hose were bagging all around her legs. The things women do to create a feminine image is crazy! This would have caused no permanent damage, as least physically. The five-inch heels on shoes that some of the women are wearing today is much more scary.

We had an English teacher who loved young people and teaching. She was quite elderly when she took the teaching position in our high school. She had the persona of a grandmother and kept a smile on her face, even in the face of some bratty kids. Why we behaved so badly I'm not sure. We acted as though she had stepped into the classroom to play with us, and she was the player who was "it." We called her Granny behind her back. I'm quite sure that she was aware of the name and she probably didn't mind it a bit. Her credentials included degrees from the University of Minnesota, Harvard as well as the University of Mexico (in English and Spanish). She had done a lot of world traveling and could have enlightened us with her experiences if we had only been more willing to listen. As an example of our awful behavior in class, one day is remembered as "the day the planes flew." When Mrs. Anderson would turn her back someone would sail a paper airplane across the room, being very careful to have his eyes focused on his book after take-off. As the classroom was used for her Spanish as well as English classes, there was a map of Mexico hanging in the front of the room. One of the airplanes managed to get its' nose stuck in the middle of the map. A hand shot up from a front row seat and Mrs. Anderson called on innocent David, a particular pet of hers. He seriously asked her if she had heard of the crash in Mexico. When she told him she had not and asked if anyone had been hurt, he told her it was a joke and pointed to the map and the crash site. She took it such rich good humor that I think that it was at that point that I finally realized that there was something very wrong with our behavior as a class and individually as students.

Our senior English classes were taught by Miss Sweeney, who taught three generations of Dawson scholars. She wore an engagement ring that she had gotten from her fiancé before he was sent overseas where he was ultimately killed in battle. She demanded and received respect from all of her students. She was another of the teachers who came to our little town and stayed. She had found and made friends, and claimed this town as hers. Obviously she had to have felt accepted and was surely considered a welcome addition to the school and community.

SMALL TOWN EXCITEMENT
Coloring Outside the Lines

⌖

There was a man who lived alone in a house, in town. We used to walk past his house on the way to the swimming pool in the summer time. I don't remember his name, but I remember being told by someone that his behavior might have been questionable. We were told, or perhaps we decided as a cautionary measure, that it would be best for us to walk on the other side of the street when we came by his house. This was at a time when we were never afraid to walk anywhere in town or outside of town, day or night. The man most likely was only reclusive and not dangerous. Being kids, we enjoyed trying to scare each other, and it must have worked, at least for a time, since it has stayed with me for all of these years.

It may seem as though we slogged through our days in a fog, not having many exciting moments in our day-to-day living. Even in a sleepy little town in the Midwest there were those of us who craved and looked for more than the humdrum, normal activities.

When I was fifteen or sixteen I became aware of the wild and wooly west in South Dakota, actually only a few miles across the state line, to a one-horse town, named Gary. There adventurous teenagers would travel to challenge the authorities who maintained law and order over the one hundred or so inhabitants. I went along with a couple of girlfriends, on a Sunday afternoon, in some male teenager's car to see if they would serve beer to young, innocent kids. We had heard that they never questioned ages of customers and we found that to be so very true. The legal drinking age in South Dakota was eighteen, versus the twenty-one age rule in Minnesota. So, here the sneakers and white bucks met the cowboy boots of our neighbors to the west. This was a pretty regular excursion for some of the kids. If the parents had been aware of what their children were doing they might have started a campaign to build a wall between the states! Obviously, this trip of thirty miles or so was a real threat to the lives of good friends in search of a good time. Hopefully, the designated driver practice was employed. Then, as now, kids are not always the best judges of safety issues. Kids have forever deemed themselves to be invincible.

It was in the fall of the year, since I remember that the night was just a little cool. Some girlfriends were hanging out on the street in town, just looking for something to do. We happened to meet one of the older girls who had a car and who was gracious enough to invite us to accompany her to Montevideo to watch the train come into the depot. This girl was more interested in cars and mechanics than pretty dresses and boys. At that time, if you didn't fit the normal mold of what was expected, you were left on your own to figure out your own way. Girls would be wise to know what to do if there was a flat tire, but it was somehow not right to actually enjoy the act. Trains didn't stop in every little town along the way, so we thought it would be fun to witness the arrival of the passenger train. As I recall, I don't remember anyone actually getting on or off, but we did have a short conversation with the station master before getting back into the car and going back the twenty miles. It was that night that I smoked my first cigarette, a Pall Mall. It tasted foul and left bits of tobacco on my lips. I would never take up that habit (or so I thought).

I had been trusted to drive the family car with only a learner's permit. We lived just three miles from town, the weather was fine and with the promise to allow only Sally to ride with me as a passenger and not to travel any farther than to town and back, we set out cruising Main. Mind you, this was a weeknight with hardly a soul around. It was around nine o'clock when on one of our trips down Main Street, we managed to get the attention of the one and only Otto, the only uniformed employee of the town. He was middle aged and took his job seriously. That is, until he began to flirt with us and had told us that although we were not yet old enough to have a driver's license, it was okay for us to drive in town as long as we obeyed all the traffic laws. Foolishly, Sally and I at the age of fifteen decided that we had permission to drive as though we had earned that right. That particular night Otto followed us to the city limits and turned on the blue lights. We came to a stop and waited for Otto to come to the driver's side window. That was when he told us that we were speeding. I don't remember the specifics, but seem to recall that he claimed we were going five or ten miles over the posted speed limit. Maybe he thought we'd cry and beg, but instead we argued with him. We knew that we weren't speeding and then he decided to write us a ticket for just that and for driving without a license! When he drove off, I took Sally to her house and dropped her off. Then I went home and by the time I entered the house I was angry and crying. How I had the courage to wake my mom and dad amazes me to this day. The fact that I reported to them that night all of the nasty doings of Otto, the town clown, must have struck a raw nerve with my dad. I was told to go to bed. The next morning my dad came to wake me up to tell me that he was taking me to school that day. As we came into town we stopped in front of the municipal judges' office and climbed those long stairs to the second floor. Apparently dad had made an early morning appointment to see the judge, and by the time dad had told him what he thought of the middle aged predator of young girls, the judge tore up the ticket and I was taken on to school. My usually quiet and law abiding dad once again displayed the other side, that of protector and loving father. I don't believe the incident was ever mentioned again at home, but I feel that word went out and justice was done. I was never told that what I did was justified, but couldn't help but feel that I would ever have to doubt that my parents would keep me safe.

Sunny Sunday afternoons in western Minnesota can be and were often very cold in the middle of winter. After tromping around town with coats, scarves, gloves and boots covering us from head to toe, we were still cold to the bone. Sally and I stopped at one of the cafes on our main street and indulged in hot chocolate with whipped cream on top. This was real cocoa, not the stuff in a jar or package like we use today. It was rich and tasted the way Mom made cocoa at home, using milk.

Another experience of winter was the time that I drove my car onto the ice at Lac qui Parle Lake. Incidentally, the Dakota Indians called this body of water "lake that speaks" because of the noise that the water birds made as they landed on the lake. The French fur traders, the first white men to enter Dakota Territory, translated the Dakota name into French, Lac qui Parle. A river and a county also are named Lac qui Parle. Access was made available to the lake by people who liked to ice fish; they'd saw a hole through the ice in order to drop their fishing lines into the water. Avid sportsmen would haul a little house onto the lake where they could stay comfortable while waiting for the fish to bite. The hole they had cut would be in the middle of the ice floor and all they had to do was drop the fishing line through the opening and wait. Here the fish house would remain until the first of the spring thaws when they would be taken back to shore. Therefore, getting out onto the lake was no problem. Once out in the open, just accelerating a little and tapping the brakes allowed you to spin and enjoy the ride. I felt that I should try this once, I guess, and it was a lot safer than other driving tricks.

Before the sport of stock car racing entered the scene locally, some of us were tempted to try drag racing. I did not get to drive the family car very often, so maybe I thought I should get the most out of the opportunity as possible. One Sunday afternoon I was driving the green Plymouth with the push button gearshift when some boys out on a paved road north of town challenged us. It was a straightaway and perfect place for a safe drag race. I do not remember who won, but I do remember that it was fun, and only later did I think about what might have happened if my parents had ever found out about it. There was only one other time that I took part in that sport. On a Sunday afternoon, on another paved country road on the opposite side of town, I was driving Dad's pickup. A boy from a nearby town was also driving a pickup truck. It seemed only natural to challenge the driver of the other truck to a drag race. He was probably more rational than we were, since, as I recall, he backed off and so ended the race.

I remember Elvis and Fats Domino on jukeboxes in all of the cafes. I recall listening to country western music when it wasn't that popular, but Sally and I liked some of the Grand Ole Opry stars and would buy the 45's and listen to them by ourselves. I can relate to being country when country wasn't cool. We used to go down to the furniture store at night. We had a key to get in to the side door and we would sit in the dark with only the street light to show us our way in the store and play our records on the phonograph players in the store. It may seem sort of silly as Sally had a really nice player at home, but I guess we thought we could be there unsupervised at the store. It wasn't as though we invited friends to be there with us; that would have been too much freedom, even for us! We listened to all types of music and enjoyed hearing instrumental, Broadway and classical music.

One day, during study hall, some of us had signed out of study hall to go to the music room. There we would sing or practice in groups for our own pleasure. On this particular day, we got caught by the music director in the band room where Sally was playing the piano and I was singing She's Only a Bird in a Gilded Cage in my best gay nineties voice. Mr. Solie appeared, applauding, and I was so embarrassed, especially when he divulged my efforts in front of the full high school choir at practice the next day. This incident resulted in my high school prophesy of being a singer in a gay nineties bar in Minneapolis.

My dad's strict upbringing by my grandparents made him almost as strict as they were when it came to telling us how to choose our friends and deciding on our curfew. I remember some friends coming to our house after dark one night. I'm sure that Dad was in bed because it was probably after nine o'clock. I wasn't allowed to leave at that time of night, but we managed to converse between the driveway and my second story bedroom window. I heard all about it the next morning.

Fall nights in high school brought homecoming and working on floats in the evenings before the game. How we ever managed to have anything presentable, I don't know and I can't remember the finished product. Since our mascot was a jackrabbit I know he was riding on the float. Fun, it was!

Some days I would like to go back and relive those days, just to make sure I did not overlook something important along the way, but I probably would not appreciate my life any more now than I did then. Obviously, we tend to forget or ignore most of the heartaches and unhappy times that we encountered. Some of those times were real, some were slightly exaggerated, and believe it or not, some could be embellished to be more truthful. Those were the good old days.

Our parents had their good old days—you know, the ones before rock 'n roll—and talked about them, and now we can tell our stories the way that we want to remember. I hope that our children and grandchildren will some day do the same. I only wish that our parents had talked more about their lives before we were born. Possibly they did, but maybe we just were not listening. Therefore, I wish they had written things down for us. I certainly remember my mother saying that she wished she had asked her mother and father more questions about their early years. I am sure that she tried to share things with us. Otherwise, I would not be able to relate stories about my grandparents before I was born. I am only afraid that I did not pay enough attention to what was said. Dad liked to tell stories and perhaps we did not listen as carefully as we should have to what he said. Mom told some stories of her younger days, too. I think that I may have thought that they were trying to tell us life lessons as bits of advice and I did not think that, as a teenager, I needed that kind of information.

BAD CAR, GOOD BROTHER

Never Buy a Car on Lake Street

❧

I am told that Lake Street, as I knew it, so many years ago, no longer exists. It used to be that there were miles along Lake Street in South Minneapolis where all you would see was used car lots with a few pizza parlors mixed in here and there. To a couple of young girls, this seemed like a likely place to find an affordable car.

Jean was one of two roommates that I had at the time. Edith was the one with more common sense and caution. Jean and I had decided that we were tired of catching buses to get to work and relying on others to get out on the weekends and choose when and where we would go. It seemed perfectly logical that we should cooperate with each other in order to buy a car. After all, we worked for the same company, so the car would be equally beneficial. We figured that the two of us could easily afford a used car if we would go into the deal together. We went to a nearby dealership and were sold this decent looking car. Since Jean was 21 and could enter into a sales contract, we purchased the car in her name, and she signed a contract to make payments on a loan. Wow! That was so easy. We took out insurance and hit the road. Well, we sort of hit the road.

The weekend came and we proudly took off after work on Friday evening headed for my home to see Mom and Dad. We got in after dark and left the car sitting in the front yard. Of course, Dad was up before we were and had a chance to look at our green Chevy. When we got up we were surprised to find Dad terribly upset. He explained his reaction in no time. Then he called my brother, Roger,

137

on the phone, putting him in charge. Roger lived with his family not far from our apartment at the time. Jean and I returned to Minneapolis on Sunday afternoon after having received strict instructions to keep our speed down and to drive with caution. Monday evening Roger accompanied us to the used car dealership. When we found the salesman who had sold us the car, Roger followed Dad's instructions in dressing down the dishonest man. Roger admonished him for selling such a poor excuse for a car to a couple of girls who had no idea of what should be looked for in a safe car. I distinctly remember his saying that we could have been killed driving a car with such bald tires. He then advised him to give us our money back or find another car for us that wasn't burning more oil than gas and one that had tires with some tread on them. We were told to look at some other cars on the lot and an agreement was reached on a suitable replacement.

Once again, a hero in the family had come to my rescue. I got a quick lesson from my Dad and my brother on how to respond to an over-zealous salesman. I'm afraid I may have learned the lesson too well, since at times I am inclined to bargain with anyone willing to listen. I did this with the neighbor who wanted to buy my trailer that my husband had bought not long before he died. I proposed that the neighbor pour a concrete pad for my carport and also a pad for an outdoor storage shed in an exchange for the trailer. This man is a mason and did a beautiful job. Others have told me that I made a good deal. I also was able to get the price down on buying the carport when I purchased the storage shed at the same time. *It doesn't hurt anyone to try to strike a bargain.* After all, the worst thing that is likely to happen is for the other person to say no.

I remember, when I was young, that implement dealers would visit my Dad on the farm trying to sell a piece of equipment. Dad would sit out in his car, talking for what seemed to be hours, to get a better offer. Sometimes the seller would yield and sometimes the new equipment would be bought from another dealer. Other times, Dad might decide not to buy from anyone that year. Most importantly, buyer and seller never left with hard feelings.

I should add that the joint ownership of the car didn't last very long. I should perhaps have realized that Jean had a hard time waking up on time in the mornings, so we did have some anxious moments over that. Jean was working a part-time job in the evenings, trying to get out of debt, and at the same time, was dating and was often out late into the night. Jean announced plans to get married and Edith and I found other roommates. I told Jean that she could keep the car and make the rest of the loan payments. The next car I would have was mine alone. I had learned that not all businesses are necessarily reputable and that it would pay to do a little homework before entering into a purchase of that size. I also learned that it's a good idea to be responsible and mindful of the maintenance of a car if you plan to get your money's worth out of one's investment. The most important thing that

I learned is that it is best not to enter into a partnership with anyone when buying an item such as a vehicle. There are too many factors that make it impossible to co-own a car and still remain friends.

MOVING ON
Acknowledging Adulthood

✺

I finally began to realize that for the first time in my life I had a voice in what was happening in my country. I was able to vote in the presidential election when JFK entered the national political scene. Like so many young people at the time, I was enamored with this handsome hero who was running for election. It seemed as though the whole country was truly interested in the outcome. We wanted to experience what it would mean to be a part of the energy that we felt during the Nixon-Kennedy debates. The idea of a Peace Corps particularly for the young men and women seemed to excite a whole generation. A feeling of unity and purpose in patriotism was in the very air that we breathed. At the time, the country was at peace and everything felt right in our world. Everyone's dream of having an easier life than our parents before us seemed a possibility.

Looking back, I know that I was naïve about a lot of things happening around me. I was never tempted by marijuana or LSD or any illegal drugs. I didn't know of anyone who experimented with any of that stuff. This happened in places like San Francisco. Though I lived in Minneapolis, a bustling metropolis, the closest I came to any scary activity was from my seat on the city bus. I rode by a small section on Washington Street traveling from my apartment in South Minneapolis to my place of work in Northeast Minneapolis. This area down by the river was known for the number of homeless and drug addicts that hung out there. This was at a time when a young girl felt safe walking from the bus to her apartment after dark. There were times when I hopped on an express bus by mistake taking me four blocks from my stop. This only meant an inconvenience of walking a little farther that day. Not a big deal!

My first job was at the offices of Durkee-Atwood, a small company that manufactured automotive parts. I was hired as a key-punch operator and worked in the only air-conditioned room in the building. For this I took a two-week course to learn the basics of these early computers. I progressed through the different aspects of the department, learning the various machines involved in billing, inventory and payrolls. Each phase required a monstrous machine for its particular function. There were six or seven of us working in this big room. If you have seen pictures of the first computers, you know what I'm talking about.

After working there for a few months, I was offered the position of accounts receivable clerk. It wasn't air-conditioned outside of the computer room, but neither was it so noisy. Those first computers put out a lot of noise and heat! Part of my new job was to take the daily receipts down to the bank downtown. Normally I would catch the bus down at the corner, go to the bank and make the deposit, cash checks for individuals and return by bus. At times the president of the company would offer to give me a ride downtown in his chauffer driven sedan. His chauffer, Charles, would pick Mr. Atwood up in the early afternoon to return him to his home, and since they passed through downtown Minneapolis on their way home, I was afforded the privilege of riding in the front seat next to Charles with Mr. Atwood making small talk in the back seat. It seems odd that I took this extra nicety in stride, but I guess I was feeling the effects of being a part of the big city life and not likely to miss an opportunity to be somehow special. One morning Mr. Atwood came to my desk bringing the key to a safe deposit box and a beaded white jewelry case. He asked that I take the case with me to the bank and leave it in the safe deposit box. He had attached a note to the outside addressed to his granddaughter and put it all in a brown paper bag. Surely there must have been someone closer to him than I who would have been more trusted to perform such a duty. It so happened that he had one child, a daughter, who they say was spoiled and who had gone through a lot of money in a divorce and child custody suit. I hope that his granddaughter didn't disappoint him.

Moving into the big city of Minneapolis from a home outside of a little town was an exciting time. I didn't realize how much fun it would be until I got there. I might have made that transition the day after high school graduation if I had known. The experience of earning my own living, sharing an apartment with a couple of girlfriends, and shopping in downtown Minneapolis after work was a great new world. Sometimes I would wander down the streets stopping in shops selling hats and gloves and trying on the hats. Sometimes, as I made the trip to the bank for work, in the afternoon, I would stop at the Fanny Farmer Candy Store at the request of some of the co-workers to buy yummy turtles or fill special requests. I soon discovered that Dayton's Department Store had a bargain basement, where if I was ambitious, I could find wonderful things on sale by going through the sales racks. I thought I was earning a decent salary, but soon realized that I had to be practical to make ends meet. One of my roommates at the time managed to get herself into debt and had to pick up a part-time job in the evenings working behind the counter of a drugstore serving ice cream and cokes. My other roommate and I would sometimes drop in while she worked and she would serve up a great chocolate shake with a shot of cherry syrup that made us believe we were eating chocolate covered cherries.

I never did understand where my roommate, Jean, found a little discount shop in the basement apartment of a little lady, but we three would go there on an evening and shop for dresses at reasonable prices, trying them on and sometimes buying an irresistible dress. Unfortunately, this sweet little lady allowed Jean to buy on credit and contributed to her financial woes.

I later worked for another family-owned operation, two brothers who had a road surfacing business during the warm months and spent the winters in Florida or some other warm climate. This lasted only through October, but I had a different list of duties. I communicated with the men out on the job by two-way radio and ran the one-girl office taking calls from prospective customers, giving simple estimates and running errands when necessary to the post office and sometimes picking up lunch from a nearby establishment.

When that job ended with the coming of winter, I found a job working for another small firm, this time a painting and decorating operation. This business on the outskirts of St. Paul housed the office of this firm and also leased an office to a drywall contractor. The atmosphere was friendly and comfortable. We had a full kitchen and would often congregate there during lunch and share a meal that someone would cook. Sometimes one of us would go to a neighborhood convenience store and get bread and cold cuts for lunch. We always had coffee ready and walked around with a cup in our hands most of the time. The partners had a contract with the biggest low-cost housing company in the twin cities at the time. We met with new home buyers so they could pick their appliances and paint and wallpaper from our catalogs. I started out in this job as an assistant bookkeeper, but ended up being the color coordinator after one of the partners was killed in a private plane crash and the remaining partner started to downsize the business. This job lasted until the surviving partner decided to close the doors. I sometimes wonder what may have happened were it not for the horrific accident that killed not only the partner, Patch, but two of his little girls, as well. Patch flew an Apache Cessna and was headed back from a spring holiday in Florida when he flew into a storm over the Everglades. His wife and third daughter returned in a commercial plane and learned his plane was missing after they had returned to their home.

My next stop was at the employment office of 3M Company in St. Paul. There I was hired to work in their cost accounting department, basically pricing new tape products as the engineers came out with new and varied tapes like the Scotch Tapes we are familiar with today. It was in the elevator on my way back from the cafeteria to the offices on the thirteenth floor that the public address system announced the shooting in Dallas of President Kennedy. Never had I seen so many people become so quiet and solemn in such a busy place. I remember that not much work was done that afternoon and what stands out in my mind was the television coverage over the next few days. I can only describe it as relentless mourning. The sadness permeated the air and, for a while, the whole country seemed numb.

This tragic time in history seemed to change the tide, at least for me. I finally began to feel the undercurrent of unease that was moving throughout the country. I honestly had no idea how real the problems were in other parts of the country. Until I moved to the South in 1967, I was wrapped in the cocoon of innocence. This is a shameful admission of my unintentional selfishness. My first reality check came when I walked into a convenience store to buy a loaf of bread. As I approached the check out counter, the man behind the register ordered the elderly black man to step aside and let me go first. My first reaction was that this old man had to have been a constant pest to the businessman, perhaps justifying the rudeness. Only later did I realize that this was not unusual and that this type of treatment was widespread. Shame on the clerk and shame on me, especially, for not speaking up and stopping this offense.

This incident happened in the same town where the integration at the University of Georgia by Charlayne Hunter and Hamilton Holmes took place six years earlier. Local people at that time were still very prejudiced, some of them quite vocally, and did not want to be told how to deal with racial issues. Even today, I cannot quite wrap my mind around the way so many distort their thinking by justifying their hate (or should I say dislike?) of blacks as a whole, but declare the love (or should I say like?) of the blacks that they have been associated with, usually in the workplace. The whole transformation of learning to live side by side with those different from one's self is a slow process. Today we have the same trust issues with the Hispanics that once was almost entirely directed at African-Americans. We consider ourselves unbiased, yet we continue to label each other by reference to color or ethnicity. Of course, to describe someone fully, we have to include things such as age, height, color and weight. But we shouldn't have to talk of everyday things in reference to others as though we are picking a person out of a police line up. To repeat a quote by someone on any subject should not have to be prefaced by an outline of their family tree or the side of the track they started from. Sometimes I think we are doing better and sometimes it seems were going backwards in our tolerance of each other.

Gradually, more and more non-white students were attending the University. Many of them were on scholastic and athletic scholarship. Sometimes I cannot help but wonder how much slower the acceptance of non-whites would have been were it not for the likes of Herschel Walker and others like him. The reddest rednecks are probably the most devoted football fans in this part of the country. If you love the sport, you must love the sports hero. I attended a lecture by Charlayne Hunter-Gault in the Performing Arts Auditorium after she had joined CNN as a correspondent. I have never seen any woman more poised than she. I became an instant admirer of her.

I was working at the University Bookstore in the seventies when long hair, short skirts and streaking were commonplace on campus. A streaker ran through the Bookstore one afternoon, but was out of sight before being identified or arrested. I was startled to learn from one of the student wives working in our office that her husband had been with a group of streakers on Baxter Street the night before. As the numbers grew the notoriety lessened and the fad dissipated. At this time, veterans from the VietNam War were coming to collect their scholarships at the University. Most were able-bodied, but some were disabled. The reality of the results of the war began to make the scene. The difference between the vets and the carefree young men and women were obvious. It would be hard to streak in a wheelchair.

❧

Before My Time

From the Land of the Midnight Sun to America

❧

I am first, and foremost, an American. I am proud to be a member of this most wonderful country in the world. Being born in the midst of a world war we were reminded of the importance of patriotism and respect for our leaders in government. My neighbors were first and second generation Americans whose families had come from Europe. There everyone was affected directly either by the takeover of their country or by the fears associated with war. From my earliest childhood memories, I have been mindful of the efforts of our founding fathers and the sacrifices that have been made by thousands of Americans throughout the course of history. The first lesson taught in the elementary school on the first day of my formal education was the Pledge of Allegiance to the flag. A flag hung outside the schoolhouse every day we were in school. Many times we stood around the flag as it was raised and saluted while we recited the pledge. Other days we stood by our desks to pledge to the smaller flag indoors. There were forty-eight stars on the flag at the time. Alaska and Hawaii came later.

My second loyalty is to my ancestry. Both sets of my grandparents were Norwegian emigrants to the United States and pledged their loyalty to the United States. They struggled to learn the English language and seemed to adjust to their adopted country with amazing ease. However, they didn't forget the country of their birth and they made it natural for us, their descendants, to maintain pride in our heritage. From my grandparents and parents my siblings and I were taught to be honest, good citizens and to work hard to make our way in the world.

Dad's Beginnings

The earliest history of my father's ancestors goes back to a farm 30 miles north of Oslo, Norway that was settled by the family in 1100 AD at Nes near the Vorma River in Romerike Fylke near what is now the Gardemoen Airport.

The Black Death or Bubonic Plague that killed off a majority of the Norwegian people caused this farm, like thousands of others, to lie idle for decades, until it was again occupied in the 1600's. On this farm, two finely carved oxen of flint were found. These were identified as having been made in the Neolithic Stone Age, 4000-4500 years ago.

The family name in the 1600's was Grimkelsrude. This was Americanized to Green.

The family can be traced in Norway from around 1700 through six generations to my grandfather, Hans, who was born in 1875 to Ole Hanson Bjornlie and Ida Alette.

Dad's mother, Gunda Hofseth, was the first of her family to come to the United States. She was just eight years old when her father died leaving her mother with her and six other children under the age of eighteen and pregnant with another child. The children went out to work in the dairy industry, the boys at the "meieri" where milk was bottled and delivered, and the girls became dairymaids. Plans were made to leave for America as soon as they saved enough money for passage. Grandma became engaged to Christian Skoien before he left for America in 1892. After he had settled in Minnesota he sent for her and they married. Together they had three daughters, Karen (Carrie), Hilda and Agnes. But sadly, when the girls were just six, four and two years old, their father died at the age of twenty-nine on February 22, 1900. Grandma's mother, Karen, still in Norway, had watched as Grandma left for America. Soon after, Grandma's sister Hannah joined her. When Grandma's first husband died, two of Grandma's brothers bought tickets for their mother, Karen, to travel with them to America. According to family history the three emigrants arrived in Madison, Minnesota by train and asked for directions of the first person they met after they left the depot. It just so happened that the person they approached was Grandma's brother-in-law who lived nearby. They were invited to spend the night with him and the next day brought them eight miles to Grandma's farm. Great-grandmother Karen lived with Grandma until she died in 1920, helping to raise eleven children.

Meanwhile, my grandfather emigrated from Norway to America and settled in Western Minnesota. He married the young widow, Gunda Skoien in 1904. My father was the first child born to this marriage. My grandparents had seven more children whom they raised in a small house on a farm. One can hardly imagine eleven children and their parents living in a house that size. The white frame house still stands to this day. If you go in and stand real still in the quiet you can almost hear the chatter of children speaking in their native tongue, and eating around the supper table the favorite dishes from the parents' homes in Norway. This would include a lot of home baked bread and cheese and dairy products along with beef, pork, chicken and eggs and of course, vegetables from the garden.

Mom's Beginnings

My mother's ancestors have been traced back to the early 1600's in Norway. Her father's family lived on a farm a few miles northwest of Hegra, Norway. The farm is along a stream where salmon fishing is good during the spring spawning season. When my grandfather immigrated with his family to America in 1865 he was just fourteen years old, the youngest of five children of John and Sarah Dahl. Included in the family who traveled together were the husbands and children of the two oldest daughters and a third daughter and the two sons. A total of thirteen people in their party sailed from TeRonde on the ship, Bergen, in 1865 and landed in Quebec, Canada. They ultimately settled in Minnesota where they all claimed their new homes.

My grandmother, Rebecca Greseth, immigrated to America in 1883 at the age of 19. She and my grandfather married in 1884. Their families probably knew each other in Norway as they lived only a few miles apart. It is speculated that their marriage may have been arranged before my grandfather left Norway, although my grandmother would have been a young girl at the time.

My grandfather homesteaded the free farmland and as he tilled the land he had been given, he began to add to his acreage as the law allowed. As a small child, I recall visiting the house my grandfather built in 1900. I felt dwarfed by the size of the rooms. This house seemed to be really elegant for its day. My grandparents had retired and moved to a house in town sometime before I was born, and when I was there as a little girl my mother's oldest brother lived there with his family. I was awed by the high ceilings, the ornate woodwork and heavy tapestry on the windows. The downstairs had a huge kitchen, walk-in pantry and tall windows letting in the sunlight on a cold winter morning. On one wall was a sink built into a counter. At the end of the sink was a pump that brought water from the cistern into the kitchen. This was the modern running water of the day. Rain water collected from the house roof eaves ran into a vast holding tank beneath the house. From the kitchen pump water would be ready for washing dishes and taking baths. Of course this running water would not be heated. The water for baths and washing dishes or clothes would be heated in the reservoir in the kitchen stove. A windmill supplied fresh water from underground for drinking for family and farm animals. This water would have had many minerals in it, which provided a good flavor, but did not pass the test for clothes washing. Rain water was much softer and made for whiter and brighter clothes!

There was also a large dining room, a living room and a cozy little parlor. The parlor had large overstuffed horsehair sofas with rich, dark reds and green colors. I have no idea how many bedrooms the house had since all but one were on the second floor. I have a feeling that my grandfather was pretty successful and the house was a matter of great pride to him.

This Victorian style house was built before my mother was born. When my grandparents on my mother's side were first married they lived in a sod house. The area in Western Minnesota was very much prairie land, and trees had to be dug up from along the river banks and transplanted on the farm to form the protective wind and snow breaks around the house and farm buildings. There seems to be an abundance of cottonwood trees, as well as elm trees and willows. Traveling to the north is like entering another country with all of the pine trees and wild berries. The story that my grandmother told her children of the first year on the prairie had to do with the Native Americans traversing to the west toward the Dakotas. My grandfather had left my grandmother at the sod house to get supplies at one of the towns that had a railroad station. The nearest town would have been a dozen miles away and traveling with horse and wagon was not a quick trip. My grandmother was expecting to see my grandfather coming home and could see for miles in all directions if she climbed unto the top of the sod house. When she did this, she saw not her husband, but a tribe of Indians going by at a distance. Not having had any contact with the natives, she was naturally very frightened. When my grandfather finally did make it home he found his wife huddled in a corner of the sod house, afraid to move or make a sound. I could be persuaded to believe that plans for a much larger house started after that.

There are many stories of these transplanted Europeans moving from old and sheltered farms and villages to the open plains. Summers, I believe, were pleasant for the most part, although the heat could be stifling. Even shade trees were not that plentiful. But the isolation in the winter months when days are short and the dark long, coupled with the extreme cold, could be almost intolerable to many. We have to remember that this was before the turn of the nineteenth century, before luxuries such as electric lights and comforts that people of today take for granted, that is until a winter storm takes out electric power and several inches, or feet, of snow makes travel an impossibility for sometimes days at a time. Then it becomes easier to appreciate the lives of our ancestors who only survived because of their determination and inner strength.

The house of my maternal grandparents had been completed, but it would be several years before my mother was born. Grandmother wanted to return to Norway to see her mother and feared that if she didn't make plans to make the trip, she would not be able to see her again. Travel had become a little easier by this time and she arranged to go to Norway and spend the summer of 1900 away from home and family. The five children ranged in age from four to fourteen at the time. The oldest were considered capable of taking care of themselves during the day while my grandfather was out in the fields.

However, I don't know who was left in charge on a hot summer day when the youngest saw the cistern pump in the kitchen as a beautiful source of water for a swimming pool. I feel sure that the older children had chores to do and may have left the others on their own for a while. They must have worked very hard to make the kitchen pump bring up enough water to cover the kitchen floor. This story was told to me by my mother, but I don't know who told it to her or the punishment that was handed out to the guilty parties. They probably felt the heat more when my grandfather got home than it had been at any time before that day.

When my grandmother came from Norway back to the farm in Lac Qui Parle County, Minnesota she brought with her a number of silver spoons. Her mother had taken her large silver ladle to a silversmith who melted it down and from it fashioned the teaspoons and tablespoons, which were later divided amongst her children. They were delicate spoons, with the year 1900 engraved on the handles. I have one of the spoons, which I value more than it will ever be worth in dollars and cents. Other antique pieces include the spinning wheel made for spinning wool into yarn, which I possess, and a sugar bowl, both of which were brought by my grandmother when she left Norway at the age of 19. Her maiden name is printed on the side of the spinning wheel as a testament of its ownership. The spinning wheel had been stored in the attic of my grandparents' farmhouse. Fortunately, Mom had the courage to go to her brother and his wife to stake her claim on it. Grandma had promised it to my mother and she to me, thus my good fortune. My sister has the trunk that traveled with my grandmother on her steamship journey to settle and marry in this country. It is probably made of pine and has a wooden, dark patina, a round top and handles on the ends.

A small section of land from my grandparents' farm was still in the estate when they died, and this forty acres of land was rented out for years afterwards. At the end of the growing season, the profits were tallied and distributed to the six heirs. Sometimes the profit was so little that it would be kept in the bank to pay taxes. After overhearing the conversations among the adults, I remember being fascinated by the references to this piece of property. When I asked Mom about it, she explained that it was just a little land. From that I surmised that it was a garden, and asked if we might go see the garden to see how it was doing. There were Sunday drives out in the country when the crops were coming up to see how the "garden" was prospering compared to other farms around. Although the proceeds were split into six shares, there were years when the portion my mother received was enough for something special. I remember one year in particular that the income was enough for new drapes for the living room and dining room. Sometime later the land was sold, marking the end of Grandpa's homestead.

My Parents Before Me
Things I Learned from my Parents

A t the time that my mother would have begun the first grade, she became very sick with rheumatic fever and had to be kept at home the first year. As she recovered, it was decided that she would be better off staying in town to attend school. The little country school where her siblings had attended was too far to walk to or ride in a wagon to in the dead of winter for her. By this time, one of her sisters, who was sixteen years older than she, had married and lived in a little town, Dawson, not far from home. As she had no children of her own, my aunt became like a second mother to my mother. She finished elementary school living with her sister and brother-in-law. By the time she was in high school my grandparents had retired from farming and had moved to a little house in town. From there, my mother went on to Normal Training School and taught elementary school in the surrounding country schools for the next eight years.

My mother said that when she finished high school, she could choose to do one of three things. She could go to nursing school, (but couldn't stand the sight of blood), she could go to Normal Training School, or she could get married. She wasn't ready for the marrying option, and since she had ruled out nursing, it was teaching for her. (After marrying and having raised five children, she probably wouldn't have seen the sight of blood as being much of obstacle.) Lois tells me that the story Mom told her about choosing a profession was that Mom wanted to go into nursing, but that her parents didn't think that nursing was as honorable a profession as teaching.

155

So many things were happening in the world as my parents were growing from adolescents to adulthood. They were beginning to see automobiles out on the country roads, even in the prairies of Minnesota. So, by the time my mother began teaching school, she had her own car that she would have to crank before she could get in it and drive. She told us her stories of teaching in one room schools to children grades one through eight. Some of the older boys were bigger than she was and didn't always behave in the way they should have. My mother was a pretty woman and dressed fashionably and nice and I'm sure some of these older boys may have had a crush on her. She tells of the cold mornings in the winter when she would have to get to school to start a fire in the pot bellied stove so that the room would have begun to warm up when the children arrived. Older children would take turns going out to get water in a pail from the well out in the schoolyard to be used for drinking water during the day. A dipper in the pail was used by all of the children. Likewise, the older boys were assigned to keep wood for the stove supplied so that everyone stayed warm during the day. Many of the years that my mother was teaching, she would board in the home of one of the families. They would provide her with a room to sleep in and she would eat with the family. I can imagine how hard it must have been to be fair to everyone in the classroom after becoming a part of one of the families' home life.

My parents were born within two months of each other and less than five miles apart in the country. Perhaps, if my mother had not been ill and sent off to go to school in the first grade, they would have shared more of their childhood. After all, they had their baby portraits made in the same photographer's studio standing on the same chair. The pictures seem to have been made of them at the same age, so they were probably in the studio a couple of months apart. Nonetheless, they didn't start to date until both of them had been out in the world, living independently, with each of them earning a living. A cousin told us just recently that he had been spending the night at our grandparents' house when my mother came home from a date with my father. My cousin was a little boy and was eavesdropping from the upstairs hall. He said my mother was so excited that her noisy exclamations of joy got his attention. Her words, according to him, were, "He asked me to marry him." I was pleased to get this little tidbit of information from my cousin. It was a story I had not heard before.

My father finished the eighth grade in a one-room school, located two miles from his parents' farm. A few stories crept out from those days. The one that I recall is of the boys playing out in the yard at recess and slipping into the Norwegian language while playing. This was not acceptable. After all, this was one of the most important reasons for being there - to be able to read and write English and get along in this country. I know that the studies in these little schools gave very basic lessons in the 'reading, riting and 'rithmetic, but these schools provided a lot of children with a love for learning and urged the appreciation of their community and country. I believe that this generation of American born citizens had as much patriotism and loyalty to their country as the founding fathers a hundred and fifty years before them.

A part of my father's history became known to my sister, and then to my brothers and me, only in recent years. My father's cousin, who has done a lot of research into her ancestry, revealed to us that another relative, a cousin to my Dad and her, was a bit of an outlaw. As I recall, the story is that cousin Anton appeared at the home of my dad's parents one day when my uncle, Reuben, was there alone. Anton claimed to need some help and so had borrowed some clothes that belonged to my dad and probably some other supplies. Later, the sheriff visited the farm looking for Anton. It seems he had stolen a car and was on the lam. His fate has never been known. Some rumors were that he had been seen in North Dakota at one time.

My parents grew up during a formative time in the United States, particularly in this area of the country. For the first time in the history of the United States, this young country, still in its adolescence, became noticed around the world as a power to be considered. When the United States entered the First World War in Europe, my mother's younger brother joined the army and fought in the front lines in France. He was in the infantry and lost a good portion of his hearing from that experience. But he came back all in one piece, except for the hearing loss, and was a dear uncle to all of us. He married shortly after he returned and it was his son who heard of the marriage proposal that he recently related to my sister and me.

Uncle Rob wrote to Mom from France describing his journey from the United States to the Argonne in France. A portion of his letter follows:

Beuvry La cote, France
Feb. 14, 1919

Dear Sister Olga,

Received your letter written January 18 and will tonight take time to send you a few lines to let you know that I am well and getting along alright.

There's moving picture show here this evening, but I have quite a few letters to write so I don't think I'll take it in. Last night I received the letter brother John wrote where he stayed in town. I am glad that he's over the flu.

See by your letter that you got the handkerchief that I sent you. I sent one each to Sina and Nora, too. Did they get them?

I have no news so I will tell you a little about my trip across. We left Camp Mills on August 7th, got on the boat in the afternoon and laid in the harbor till the next day. Left New York harbor about four o'clock August 8 and were thirteen days on the ocean. Arrived at Liverpool, England the 21st about ten o'clock in the morning. Got off the boat in the afternoon and marched to the railroad station. It was there I sent card or greeting from King George. We left Liverpool the same day and arrived at Winchester at midnight and hiked three miles to a resting camp. Stayed there two days and hiked back to town again and boarded the train and rode for three hours, arrived at South Hampton and stayed there half day. Got on a boat again, left there in the evening and when I woke in the morning we were at Havre, France. We got off the boat early in the morning and hiked three or four miles to a resting camp again. Stayed there for a day and hiked back to Havre and were loaded in box cars and rode for three days and four nights. Talk about a stiff neck when we got off the train. We could hardly walk. We got off the train early in the morning and our cooks built a fire and made some corn beef stew. After break-

fast we rested till about nine o'clock and put on our packs and hiked all day about twelve miles and arrived at San Coires that evening. We stayed there three weeks. It was there that I picked so many blackberries that I told you about. We drilled every day while we were there.

I left San Coires September 16th, hiked one day and were loaded on box cars again and rode for two days and two nights. Got off the train in a town that had been shot up by the Germans. We camped back in some woods about half a mile from town. That day as soon as it got dark we started hiking. See, we were in the war zone so we could not hike in daylight any more. We hiked about four miles that night and camped in woods again during the day. Hiked for three nights before we got to the outfit we were attached to. The second night we hiked we could hear the guns on the front. We got to the outfit that I am with now the 21st of September, a few days before the big Argonne drive started. Guess I told you about it, didn't I?

I'll never forget the night of September 26th. I was doing guard duty tht night and had just been relieved and gone to bed when the Germans started to send over some shells and we all got into the trenches, after the shells stopped coming over and I was going to bed again we got ordered to roll packs and be ready to move at once. We got ready and started to move when our big guns opened up.

This is where the letter leaves off. Apparently, the last page or pages of the letter were somehow lost. The letter had been written in pencil on lined note paper, making it hard to read with the passage of time. However, we are aware that Uncle Rob took part in some of the most dangerous and crucial battles of World War I, losing much of his hearing because he was so close to the big guns. He was a hero, though a modest one. He loved to bird hunt and would take my older brothers with him to tramp through the woods looking for game. My brothers loved to see him get out of his car with his rifle. He often supplied shells for the boys' guns.

My father and his two brothers were too young to enter the war and luckily for all of us, they were beyond the draft age when the United States entered the Second World War. Dad registered at the draft board, but was refused for service because he had had yellow jaundice. That, flat feet or claiming to be a conscientious objector seemed to be the reasons for not qualifying for the draft at the time.

My father left his parents' farm and rented a farm just a few miles from there. The house had been occupied previously by a family who had two sons. One of the sons was killed while the two of them were out together hunting. The rumor was, it is said, that the brothers had been quarrelling and the question arose about whether or not one of the brothers may have deliberately shot the other. As I understand it, there was only speculation as to what lead up to the shooting and no one was accused of any wrongdoing.

At any rate, my father swore that while he was living alone he would lay in bed at night and hear the door from the outside open and close and then hear footsteps going up the stairs to the second floor. He told us that he thought the murdered brother was coming home to sleep in his room at night. To make the story more believable, Dad told us that he would hear the sound of footsteps as they came back down the stairs in the early morning hours and leave the house in the same manner that he entered. The way we heard it, this practice was repeated night after night. My father was a good storyteller and we always disputed his story, but he insisted it was the truth and we delighted in the excitement of the ghost story and begged to hear it over and over again.

The depression was at its peak when my parents were married. Fortunately, they had no debt, and so, only struggled to maintain some stability. Their first year of marriage tested their ability to work together. My oldest brother would be born in May 1935, but during one of the coldest nights of that winter, my parents woke to the smell of smoke. A chimney fire had broken out. Quickly, my mother threw on clothes and went out to crank the car and, in the process, lost one of her mittens. After several attempts, the car did start and she drove to the house of her sister and brother-in-law who had a telephone. Unfortunately, she missed the driveway leading to their house, the car ended up in the ditch in the snow, and she had to abandon the car and walk the remainder of the way to her sister's house. She woke them and they called the fire department. The nearest fire department was twelve miles away, so, by the time they got there, the house had pretty much burned to the ground. Neighbors who had seen the flames or been alerted came to help, but not before my father had moved a heavy oak buffet filled with my mothers best dishes, the oak dining table and other big pieces of furniture out onto the snow on the lawn. Later, my father tried to lift the buffet and couldn't move it, but the adrenaline running through him that night gave him the strength to carry it out by himself and without breaking a single cup or plate! Amazingly, neither of them was injured and they became parents for the first time when my oldest brother was born. When we asked what happened to the ghost, Dad said he didn't hear him after the house burned down. Whether he burned down with the house or left when his home was gone, we couldn't surmise. This added more excitement to the ghost story that we begged to hear over and over again.

The year was 1935, and the landowner that my parents rented from built a new house on the site of the one that had burned. In the meantime, Mom and Dad lived in the garage. I have a faint recollection of the location of the garage, but not a clear picture of the way it looked. Not having any pictures of the house that burned down, I can only presume that the new house was a big improvement over the old one. This, my parents' second home, is the home of my earliest recollection. We always entered by the back door. Three steps ahead took us to the kitchen door. Coming in from outside there were stairs immediately to the right that lead to the basement. I remember a baby bottle being dropped, by my mother, and breaking on the concrete floor at the bottom of the basement steps when it fell. I can still see a rocking horse in the basement, a strange recollection, but for some reason, that's where I see it in my memory.

Around the corner to the right in the kitchen were the stairs leading to the second floor bedrooms. The green wood-burning stove occupied the space on one wall and next to it the door that led to the master bedroom. Of course, there was always the wood box that stood next to the kitchen stove. It was a big box with a hinged lid, probably three cubic feet square. This was kept filled at all times, a chore for little people. This box followed us from one house to the next. With the replacement of the green wood-burning stove with the new electric range, there was no need for the wood box in the kitchen. My sister reminds me that the big green box served as a receptor of cold weather gear on the back porch. Here mittens and scarves for outdoor play were stored, ready for the next winter. My mother was more than likely happy to see it disappear from the kitchen, but in the habit of being forever thrifty, she would find still another use for the box!

The other rooms downstairs were the dining room and living room. The living room held an overstuffed sofa and chair and my mother's upright piano, the gift from her parents for her high school graduation. A door from the dining room led to the screened in, front porch. This is where I spent a lot of time playing with baby dolls and paper dolls. It also held my mothers Singer Sewing Machine with the foot pedal. It had the features of the drop- down storage and the cover on hinges that would serve as a worktable extension, when in use, and, flipped over, it changed into a table. The pedal swung up and under a shelf. Magically, the sewing machine became an occasional table!

The house sat on a knoll slightly above the farm buildings. This farm serves as the basis for what a farm should be, in my mind. Isn't it strange that the mind of a small child would retain such insignificant details and that these ideas would have such a lifelong effect on one? Quite possibly there may have been many defects or imperfections on this farm that I was not aware of, but that's one of the advantages of being an innocent child. My only prayer is that all children could feel as loved and safe as we felt growing up.

EPILOGUE
Traveling Back

The past week has reminded me of how fickle the mind can be. The state of mind obviously affects ones' memories far beyond our wishes. While the mind protects us when necessary to maintain our sanity, at the same time we can so easily lose parts of our lives that we would like to remember. On the other hand, snapshots of our lives can live on and on, and seem never to lose their lucidity.

My sister, Lois, and I went back to visit the farm where we lived when I was between the ages of six and nine. Lois was not yet four when we left and has virtually no memory of that time in our lives. The closer we got to where I remembered the farm to be, the less I expected to find the home that I remembered. The community that I knew had changed drastically in the last sixty years or more since I had been there. Many of the small farms, or rather, I should say farm buildings, had disappeared and had been replaced with cornfields and soybean fields. However, when we approached the site from a half mile away, I saw the slight rise where the schoolhouse had stood across the drive from our farm. The schoolhouse was gone and in its place was a cornfield.

Much to my delight, I recognized the house where I spent three years of the most carefree time of my life. My mind filled with memories of playing out in the playhouse under the trees, although the pine trees that formed the perimeter of it were gone. The granary still stood, and although the big door was tightly closed, I could see my two older brothers in the open doorway with the bows and arrows they had just made; the bow formed from a willow branch and strung with twine, the arrows from split wooden shingles.

The grove where apple trees produced the most wonderful huge, red apples—the juiciest I have ever bitten into—no longer had apple trees, only other trees, but I could see just where the best apple tree had been, and I could nearly wish it into being there once more. The silo looked lonely. The red barn was long gone, replaced by thistles and grass. Of course, the windmill was not to be seen. In its place was a well, barely noticed in the overgrown yard. Where once the area between the house and outbuildings was worn by traffic, it was obvious from the tall grass that nobody had been around in a while.

In spite of the changes I witnessed, the house itself was easily recognized. Granted, a few changes had been made. The roof is now a tin roof where it was wood shingles. The exterior had been covered with white vinyl siding, replacing the wood plank siding, and an awning hung over the entrance to the kitchen. There is now a small wooden deck on one side, and an addition of a room appears on the back of the house next to the living room. But it was fundamentally the same house. Someone had lived there recently, though likely not since spring. Grass and weeds had taken over the ground and the driveway was a path through the weeds. The fence and gate that surrounded the house had been gone, apparently, for quite some time. Perhaps there were no chickens there to invade the area around the house. Oh, I remember every foot of the house and buildings where we lived such a short time, many years ago. It's probably for the best that we couldn't gain entry into the house. I like to keep the pictures intact, remembering the way it was when I lived there with my parents and brothers and sister. Things may have been a struggle in those days, but, as children, we were unaware of the problems our parents faced.

A day or two later, Lois and I spent part of an afternoon drinking tea with our cousin, Aletrice. Being with her is always a time of recalling the past. We asked her about the dates of her marriages. The first marriage ended abruptly when her husband developed a brain tumor and died when he was still a young man. Aletrice was left with a small child, Jon, but she married again. She and Lois mentioned that I had sung at her second wedding. I thought that they were both mistaken as I have no recollection of that. We asked Aletrice if she had family pictures that she would share with us. She brought out several albums. Among them was an album of her wedding. Among the photos of her wedding is one of me, the singer at her wedding. I sat in disbelief at this revelation. Later, after giving it much thought, I realized that her wedding followed closely the death of my dad. I had somehow erased a period of time from my memory. I still don't know what songs I sang. In retrospect, I remembered that I experienced the same memory loss after my son, Chris, died. The three or four days spent in Charleston, S.C. with my daughter Tracy and granddaughters Sarah and Rebekkah suffered the same consequences. They are not a part of my conscious past. I realize that I lived through those times doing normal things and hopefully acting normal, but I have no real memories of those times. I feel fortunate to have been able to spread my grief out over time, so was not overwhelmed. I can accept the waves that wash over me from time to time and can grab happy memories as they come. The mind is a curious thing.

GLOSSARY

blod klub: Potato dumplings made with the addition of animal blood.

bullhead fish: A brown fish with whiskers similar in appearance to a catfish; found in bottoms of small rivers and streams.

emigrate: To leave a place and go to live in another place or country.

flax seeds: The seed from the harvested flax, used in linseed oils.

gentling: The act of taming a horse after it has been broken. To make the horse or pony ready for a novice rider or child; teaching the horse to neck rein.

gooseberry: A sour berry which grows wild and sour used in preserves and jellies.

grain elevator: A storehouse for grain, where farmers bring the grain in trucks to be weighed and cleaned for sale to processors.

hay mow: Upper floor of the barn, a hay loft for storage of hay.

Homemakers' Club: An organization in the community of all women who were interested in learning new skills, a monthly meeting or social gathering held in the homes of the members.

immigrate: To settle in a new country

klub: Dumplings made with finely diced potatoes, flour, salt and pepper, sometimes with meat added.

Ladies' Aid: Ladies Aid Society in the Lutheran Church. An organization for the women in the church who do missionary work and serve the church.

lefsa: A soft traditional Norwegian flatbread made with flour, milk or cream and potatoes and cooked on a griddle.

lyceum programs: Special events in the school auditorium such as concerts, lecture and entertainment. An enhancement to the normal routine of the school.

pen pal: Two people who become friends by writing to each other and who may never meet.

rubbernecks: Persons rudely listening in on conversations during the early twentieth century when telephone party lines were common.

silage: Corn cut and chopped to be stored in silos for winter feed.

sweeping compound: A dry powdered mixture spread on the floor to control the dust during sweeping, used in schools in the mid twentieth century.

NORWAY-HERITAGE
HANDS ACROSS THE SEA
PASSENGER LISTS
SHIPS / GENEALOGY

Passenger list 1865 - bark **Bergen**

#	Name	Age	Sex	Relation
258	Kierstine Thorstensdatter Boraas*	32	f	his wife
259	Ane Marie Eliasdatter Boraas*	3	f	his daughter
260	Thorine Eliasdatter Boraas*	9mo.	f	his daughter
261	%Dorthea% %Eliasdatter%	%f%	%f%	%Servant%
262	Niel Nielsen Budstaden	22	m	Servant
263	Andreas Thoresen Dahl	53	m	Farmer
264	Sahra Hansdatter Dahl*	52	f	his wife
265	Ingeborganna Andersdatter Dahl*	3	f	his daughter
266	John Lassesen Dahl	53	m	Farmer
267	Sahra Hansdatter Dahl*	52	f	his wife
268	**Hans Johnsen Dahl***	13	m	his son
269	Sirri Johnsdatter Dahl*	18	f	his daughter
270	Jens Olsen Dahlsaunet	31	m	Farmer
271	Kierstine Larsdatter Dahlsaunet*	35	f	his wife
272	Hans Olsenl! Dahlsaunet*	10	m	his son
273	Lorentz Jensen Dahlsaunet*	18mo.	m	his son
274	Marit Pedersdatter Kjerkeby	33	f	Servant
275	Ole Ahlesund	5	m	her son
276	Rollang Larsen Grønseth	33	m	Servant
277	Iver Larsen Grønseth	29	m	Servant
278	Ole Iversen Hofstad	22	m	Servant

New York Passenger Lists, 1820-1957 record for Gunda Hansen

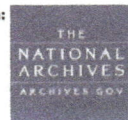

Record Index

Name:	Gunda Hansen
Arrival Date:	6 Oct 1890
Birth Year:	abt 1873
Age:	17
Gender:	Female
Ethnicity/Race-/Nationality:	Norwegian
Place of Origin:	Norway
Port of Departure:	Copenhagen, Denmark and Norway
Destination:	United States of America
Port of Arrival:	New York
Port Arrival State:	New York
Port Arrival Country:	United States
Ship Name:	Thingvalla
Search Ship Database:	Search the Thingvalla in the 'Passenger Ships and Images' database

Source Information

Record URL: http://search.ancestry.com/cgi-bin/sse.dll?h=8657267&db=nypl&indiv=try

Source Citation: Year: *1890*; Arrival: *New York, United States*; Microfilm Serial: *M237*; Microfilm Roll: *M237_556*; Line: *2*; List Number: *1489*.

Source Information: Ancestry.com. *New York Passenger Lists, 1820-1957* [database on-line]. Provo, UT, USA: Ancestry.com Operations, Inc., 2010.

Original data:

- Passenger Lists of Vessels Arriving at New York, New York, 1820-1897; (National Archives Microfilm Publication M237, 675 rolls); Records of the U.S. Customs Service, Record Group 36; National Archives, Washington, D.C.

- Passenger and Crew Lists of Vessels Arriving at New York, New York, 1897-1957; (National Archives Microfilm Publication T715, 8892 rolls); Records of the Immigration and Naturalization Service; National Archives, Washington, D.C.

1910 UNITED STATES FEDERAL CENSUS

HANS BJORNLIE

AGE IN 1910: 34
BIRTH YEAR: 1876
BIRTHPLACE: NORWAY
HOME IN 1910: LAC QUI PARLE, LAC QUI PARLE, MINNESOTA
RACE: WHITE
GENDER: MALE
IMMIGRATION YEAR: 1893
RELATION TO HEAD OF HOUSE: HEAD
MARITAL STATUS: MARRIED
SPOUSE'S NAME: GUNDA S BJORNLIE
FATHER'S BIRTHPLACE: NORWAY
MOTHER'S BIRTHPLACE: NORWAY

DEPARTMENT OF COMMERCE AND LABOR. BUREAU OF THE CENSUS
THIRTEENTH CENSUS OF THE UNITED STATES: 1910 POPULATION

SOURCE INFORMATION: WWW.ANCESTRY.COM DATABASE: 1910 UNITED STATES FEDERAL CENSUS DETAIL: YEAR: 1910; CENSUS PLACE: LAC QUI PARLE, LAC QUI PARLE, MINNESOTA; ROLL: T624_709; PAGE: 10A; ENUMERATION DISTRICT: 0063; IMAGE: 339; FHL MICROFILM: 1374722.

1910 UNITED STATES FEDERAL CENSUS

HANS J DAHL

AGE IN 1910: 58
BIRTH YEAR: 1852
BIRTHPLACE: NORWAY
HOME IN 1910: CERRO GORDO, LAC QUI PARLE, MINNESOTA
RACE: WHITE
GENDER: MALE
IMMIGRATION YEAR: 1865
RELATION TO HEAD OF HOUSE: HEAD
MARITAL STATUS: MARRIED
SPOUSE'S NAME: REBECKA DAHL
FATHER'S BIRTHPLACE: NORWAY
MOTHER'S BIRTHPLACE: NORWAY

THIRTEENTH CENSUS OF THE UNITED STATES: 1910 POPULATION.

SOURCE INFORMATION: WWW.ANCESTRY.COM DATABASE: 1910 UNITED STATES FEDERAL CENSUS DETAIL: YEAR: 1910; CENSUS PLACE: CERRO GORDO, LAC QUI PARLE, MINNESOTA; ROLL: T624_709; PAGE: 5A; ENUMERATION DISTRICT: 0064; IMAGE: 353; FHL MICROFILM: 1374722.

BJORNLIE FAMILY TREE

Ole Hans Bjornlie 1832-

Ida Alette 1851-

Hans Hansen 1840-1881

Karen Amundson 1841-1920

John L. Dahl 1809-1884

Sarah Fossen 1814-1885

Rollaug Greseth 1821-1898

Ingebord Hofstad 1818-1903

Hans Bjornlie 1875-1957

Gunda Hansen 1873-1965

Hans Dahl 1851-1940

Rebecca Greseth 1864-1943

Olaf Bjornlie 1903-1959

Olga Dahl 1904-1977

Elnora Dahl

Hannah Dahl

John Dahl

Robert Dahl

Sina Dahl

Gladys Bjornlie

Clara Bjornlie

Hilda Skoien

Agnes Skoein

Carrie Skoein

Harold Bjornlie

Inga Bjornlie

Sylvia Bjornlie

Priscella Bjornlie

Reuben Bjornlie

Roger Carlyle Bjornlie 1937-1982

David Hans Bjornlie 1937-

Wanda Bjornlie Coley 1939-

Paul Olaf Bjornlie 1942-2011

Lois Bjornlie Larson 1944-

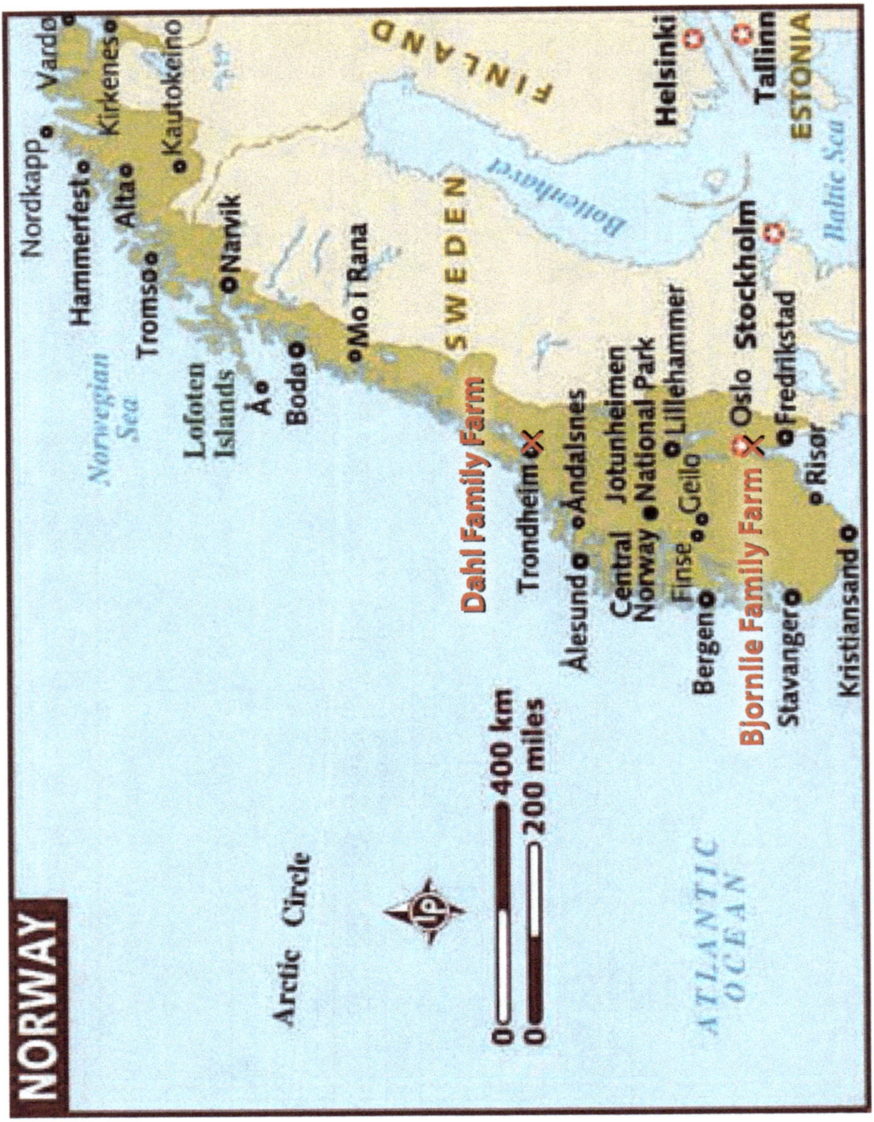
NORWAY
Nordkapp
Vardø
Hammerfest
Kirkenes
Alta
Kautokeino
Tromso
Narvik
Norwegian Sea
Lofoten Islands
Å
Bodø
Mo I Rana
FINLAND
SWEDEN
Bottenhavet
Helsinki
Tallinn
ESTONIA
Baltic Sea
Stockholm
Dahl Family Farm
Trondheim
Åndalsnes
Ålesund
Central Norway
Jotunheimen National Park
Lillehammer
Oslo
Fredrikstad
Finse
Geilo
Bergen
Bjornlie Family Farm
Risor
Stavanger
Kristiansand
Arctic Circle
0 400 km
0 200 miles
ATLANTIC OCEAN

www.ingramcontent.com/pod-product-compliance
Lightning Source LLC
Chambersburg PA
CBHW060048100426
42742CB00014B/2740